BASKETBALL: COACHING AND PLAYING

Photo: The Soldier Magazine

Amateur Basketball Association National Senior Championship 1968:
Aldershot Warriors vs Oxford University

BASKETBALL:
COACHING AND PLAYING

edited by

B. JAGGER

with illustrations by

W. LANGSTAFFE

FABER AND FABER LTD

3 Queen Square

London WC1

First published in 1962
by Faber and Faber Limited
3 Queen Square London WC1
New and revised edition 1971
Reprinted 1973
Printed in Great Britain by
Latimer Trend & Company Ltd Plymouth
All rights reserved

ISBN 0 571 04743 2

CONTENTS

CONTENTS

ILLUSTRATIONS

9

1

THE BASKETBALL COACH

by B. JAGGER

What sort of people are basketball coaches? This is a question which has many answers, for coaches are of all types and range through many degrees of personality. Consequently we find in their ranks the happy, the serious, the apparently lighthearted, the single-minded, the experimenters, the young and the experienced. Every coach contains this mixture in varied proportions and, according to the make-up of his personality, so will be the team he produces.

He must definitely possess certain qualities, however, and these include a sense of vocation, a dedication to the game, faith in his own ability, knowledge and enthusiasm. Attributes such as these cannot easily be tested by any simple yardstick but nevertheless they are all important, and unless they are definitely present and well to the fore, the team produced by the coach will be an ordinary run-of-the-mill affair, rising to no great heights and probably keeping warm the lower half of some league table. The coach who is enthusiastic and full of quiet confidence will impart these qualities to his team, and as a result the team will become a lively, spirited and knowledgeable machine. A coach of good standing will gain the respect and win the appreciation of his group, and will maintain his office because the team, through a genuine and sincere desire, want him to continue as their coach. The relationship between coach and players should be of this order and the degree of influence he exercises should be of this type.

The good coach is much more than a basketball instructor for consciously or subconsciously he assumes the role of an educationalist carrying his influence far beyond basketball itself. Many of his team will be in ordinary repetitive jobs and, to such players, basketball may have become not just a main item of recreation but a major interest in life. Their respect for the coach will be shown by a deliberate imitating of his attitude and personality, and the players in some ways will tend to reflect his outlook. These results can often be easily recognized, for the noisy coach produces a noisy team and the timid coach produces a group of players uncertain of their movements or unchecked and individually arrogant, and so on. The real coach, working true to his job, should see in his duties not only the production of an efficient team but also an educational force which broadens horizons and imparts a sense of fair play and endeavour to the youngsters under his charge. The game of basketball in the hands of such a person can become a power for good of the highest importance, consequently it is essential that the coach sets by example high standards in effort, endeavour, manners, behaviour and outlook.

BASKETBALL BOOKS

The coach, however, is a specialist and his speciality is basketball. He must to an extent be steeped in the game, always planning for improvement in his methods and approach, and continually seeking new knowledge. He must read widely but at the same time he must be wise and discriminating regarding the ideas and schemes he intends to use. The bulk of the reading material in basketball is American in origin and although excellent in many ways a great deal of it is written by high-level coaches for teams far beyond the present stage of ability in this country. Moreover, the American coach usually works to a particular system of play formulated as a result of long years of experience. He becomes known for his method and his team is fitted and adapted to his system. His players are, however, of the highest excellence and the right materials for the type of play which the coach has adopted. They are fully capable of making the system work successfully. In contrast our own players are 'beginners' and cannot successfully imitate many schemes of play put forward as commonplace by American writers.

American books on general principles of basketball are initially of considerable value but here again discrimination must be exercised in their use. The books contain a straightforward and useful description of fundamentals, but when it comes to set plays, there is usually insufficient explanation to show the difficulties of a movement or the coaching points necessary to eradicate faults. Information of this sort is not necessary for American readers, yet it is essential for their counterparts in England. The whole of the coaching pattern in America is vastly different from our own, for their wealth of experience in the game makes for well-organized and comprehensive lessons right from the earliest stages. From the beginnings of play at junior level the young American travels through an orderly system of training based almost completely on fundamentals. His grounding in the principles of the game is thorough and the whole of his upbringing is on planned lessons. Fundamentals and methodical work become regular features of his learning and his play. The result is that all players obtain training in organization and game development as well as in playing, consequently it is easy at a later date for the good player to become a useful coach. He copies the methods of training in which he was brought up and adds the wealth of his experience and the ability he has acquired. In contrast, basketball coaching in England varies from energetic game work-outs which may be merely recreative play, to the organized and progressive coaching suggested on the well-planned courses, run by the Amateur Basketball Association.

Through this welter of American books, the coach should tread warily. He would be well advised not to purchase too many, but he should consider obtaining a sound book on fundamentals, a book devoted to drills or having specialist chapters on drills and a not too advanced book on tactics and team plays. Books of this type will assist him to formulate his own ideas and his own elementary methods of play. They will give him food for thought and probably inspiration for the more effective development of his team.

PSYCHOLOGY

The all-round coach must make further additions to his knowledge and these include such things as an understanding of psychology, of hygiene and the mechanics of movement. The psychological aspect cannot be over-emphasized and the coach will acquire this from his keen observation and his understanding of the players. Within the team he will hope to have one or two stars, but for the rest there may be a great similarity between the general playing ability. There are other things to be considered, however, for although there is similarity of playing skills, this will not usually apply to personality and character. The coach should quickly recognize the stronger and sounder personalities in his unit and make the proper use of them. Players of this type are more reliable and continue to be hard workers whatever the state of the game. A team is fortunate if it possesses players of this category and the wise coach will bear in mind these characteristics when substitutions are being made. Whenever the score margin is narrow, the stronger personalities on court usually show more virility in fighting to overtake their opponents or to increase the scant lead. The flamboyant players accept a lead with delight and often rapidly increase it and thus appear to be gaining the greater glory.

Further aspects of psychology may seem to be merely common sense, for the good coach knows the right approach to each particular player and the correct way to urge all to supreme efforts. He has the knowledge also to give fair and just praise to the members of his team so that the players come away from practice or a game with a sense of satisfaction but, none the less, a determination to improve.

REACTION TO PLAY

The coach must train himself to develop a keen analytical sense when he is watching a match : his attitude must be entirely different from that of the spectator or the player. To the coach, a game is an endless succession of tactics, a demonstration of individual and team skill and understanding. The players are for the whole time examples of the coach's skill and ability. He has trained and developed them to be able to cope with all aspects of general play and to be adaptable to different methods and tactics shown by the opposition. Very few players purposely let their team or their coach down, so any apparent weakness a player shows on court may be due to a lack of understanding, or to the presence of a greatly superior adversary. The coach must help this understanding, he must quickly eradicate weaknesses and use to the full the strong points of his players. Obviously the coach rejoices in the success of his team, but he must always be ready to learn from failure as well as from success. A much more careful analysis is necessary after the team loses, for it is all too easy to apportion blame away from the right places, resulting in a wrong emphasis in training during subsequent practice sessions. Above all the coach must avoid open grumbling at a player or a team which has done badly, immediately the game is over, for this discredits the whole club. The situation is made even worse if the coach lowers himself to make direct attacks on the officials, the supporters or the general conditions for the game. This does not mean that the coach is a passive individual accepting everything meekly. On the contrary he must be robust and prepared to be critical, demanding the highest standards in his own club and willingly accepting little less at other places. His criticisms, however, must be considerate and fair and once he has accepted certain conditions at the beginning of a game then further grumbling about these aspects must cease. If objections have to be made, they should be made to the League Committee in the right way and employing the proper constitutional methods.

TEACHING ABILITY

These various attributes of coaching are of little use, however, if the coach himself has no knowledge of the elementary principles of teaching. All too often a coach considers that his playing ability and his close connection with the game are sufficient to justify him and he tends to poke fun at the teacher who is attempting to develop a team from lesser experience of play but from a greater ability in actual teaching. Every coach must be capable of imparting his knowledge and, if he does this in a planned, original and efficient way, then he has made himself into a teacher. There must be method and variety, however, in his approach and careful planning in the organization of his lessons; in addition, almost as much thought must be given to the presentation of the material as to the compilation of the material itself.

Some confusion may exist between the terms 'teaching' and 'coaching'. It is usually accepted, however, that there is a great deal of similarity between the meaning of the two words, but the teacher is attempting to put over something new and the coach by dint of practice and repetition is polishing up some skill or movement already partly known. Consequently the coach is at one time teacher and at another time coach, and he shifts from one role to the other without changing his approach, his technique or his style.

It is essential, as we have seen, that he should know basketball and that he should be capable of planning a programme of instruction. His task of conveying his thoughts and ideas to a group of youngsters or to an established team is best done by what is known as the whole-part-whole method. In this way the player is given first of all a complete picture of the actual fundamental or movement; the action is then analysed and practised in sections if this is necessary, and finally the whole movement is again practised and is carried out at game speed under game conditions. The coach must vary the use of this method to a degree consistent with the ability and age of his team, and he should take it upon himself to coach both groups of beginners and experienced players. In this way he will become aware of the high importance of correct practice and correct play in the early stages of learning, for he will see members of his experienced group who will fall short of becoming really good players due to established faults in play which cannot be eradicated.

Teaching the beginner is perhaps more important than coaching the adult, for the basis of greatness in basketball is laid during the first course of lessons. The coach will usually find that the group of youngsters under his charge are willing and keen to learn this new game of basketball. Herein lies strength and weakness, for the group may be more anxious to play than to master the fundamentals. To youngsters there is the apparent contrast between the freedom and pleasure of movement and the learning and repetition of skills. The child prefers the former but the coach knows that the latter is all-important. The gap must be bridged and the coach can do this by making the early practices as interesting as possible and by striving to understand the difficulties in performance experienced by his young players.

METHODS OF INSTRUCTION

A good approach is for the coach to give a brief explanation of a fundamental and then demonstrate it in as near perfect form as possible. The players now try out the whole movement. Many of these youngsters having seen a good demonstration will imitate the movement quite successfully, so it is essential that the demonstration should be excellent. It is a duty of the coach to be continually polishing up his performance of fundamentals, and if he feels that he has shortcomings here, then he should use the best player he can get hold of as a demonstrator, or show the actual movement on film. If the attempts made by the players at the whole movement are good, then practice should continue with the coach giving individual attention to each player and correcting major faults. The faults will be peculiar to the individual and will have been caused through lack of understanding, bad muscular control, bad co-ordination, excessive nervous tension or a mixture in varied proportion of these defects. It is the job of the coach to understand the difficulties of each player so that faults are quickly corrected before they become established. The actual correction is not always easy for the fault may be very obvious, but the reason for the fault, deep-seated. For instance, a player with a curious arm action in a jump shot may be behaving in this way because he is off balance, or in a wrong stance, or not sufficiently relaxed or confident, etc. Merely correcting the arm action will do nothing to improve these other aspects.

In these early periods of learning, the coach will quickly seek to establish the proper rhythm and the proper speed of execution in the movement. The next stage is to fit the particular fundamental into a game phase so that the player can understand the environ-

ment in which the movement is used and appreciate some of the
further difficulties associated with actual play.

If, for example, the chest pass was traced through these various
stages, the coach would follow a pattern of the following type
with his players.

(*a*) Brief explanation of pass,

(*b*) Demonstration,

(*c*) Practice by players, and individual correction by coach,

(*d*) Development of pass until action is done at the varied
speeds demanded in the game,

(*e*) Passing in game phases:

    (*i*) Passing on the move and on the run,

    (*ii*) Faking and passing,

    (*iii*) Passing against opposition, tight marking and loose
marking.

1. Chest pass, emphasizing finger follow through

It can never be expected that the teaching and coaching of a
fundamental or a new skill will proceed without any setbacks,
for many potentially good players have not the physical ability
to imitate correctly the actions of the coach. Where a fundamental
has been demonstrated and the group as a whole find real difficulty
in performance, it is wrong policy to repeat the demonstration and
then hope that all will be well. The demonstration has obviously
been useful, for the players have seen the whole movement and
they realize the end in view, but the action must now be broken
down and practised in its various parts. This makes for simplicity of movement and allows the slower players to acquire,
by degrees, the necessary skill. In this way, a lay up shot may be
synthesized to the following movements:

(*a*) Player in standing position, close to and at an angle to backboard; shot is made with correct arm action from the standing position,

(*b*) Player in similar stance to position in (*a*) but he now takes one step forward and repeats the movement of the shot,

(*c*) Player practises the movement of (*b*) but jumps high and shoots.

(*d*) Player runs forward dribbling the ball and repeats the movement of (*c*),

(*e*) Player works against opposition.

(*f*) Individual coaching is now given so that the speed of the run up is improved, the height of the jump is increased and the position of balance on landing is corrected.

This approach to instruction is still that of the whole-part-whole method for the players have seen the total movement, they have then gone on to practise it in its various parts and finally have come back to the complete movement in an aspect of the game.

Coaching and practice must never become purely mechanical and repetitive. The players must be striving to improve and the coach himself must always be trying to understand why his players react in such a way that they commit faults. From this basis of understanding, help must be given to eradicate their faults. The various practices set by the coach must be interesting, for the young player will become bored if there is neither satisfaction nor pleasure in practice. The acquisition of skill takes time and there are very few players who will achieve a high degree of all-round ability unless there is someone to help and encourage them. This does not mean that there will be boredom in playing basketball, for the game itself is always exciting, but there may be a strong desire to play and no stomach for practice if the practice itself is not purposeful and interesting. To be a good basketball player, one certainly must play, but to be a better player, practice goes hand in hand with play.

FUNDAMENTALS IN GAME PHASES

With beginners, the coach should never teach anything in isolation, for each aspect is related to the previous movement and to the subsequent movement in the game phase. He must therefore make his players aware of the background of the game and train them in general habits of play. As soon as any fundamental or movement can be done with a certain amount of precision, the environment of the game should be introduced so that play proceeds under game conditions. Certain actions must become instinctive so that quick assessments of free playing space can be made. The beginner must be trained to become an alert player capable of judging when to move to receive a pass, and where to pass the ball to the best advantage. Young players tend to work in isolation, concentrating all attention on ball possession, and this is usually because the environmental aspects of play have never been taught. Play assessment starts when beginners are coached to be aware of the whole court and this is done by developing what is known as peripheral vision, a new technique to the majority of youngsters. By habit, people tend to focus their vision directly ahead of them and the actual focal point may be on a relatively small object such as the particular single letter which is being written or the word that is read. It is difficult for youngsters to change this habit from concentrated vision to wide vision, but practice from early stages will soon make players aware of a large section of the court. Having seen the environment, their developing basketball judgement will provide the answer for the best movement. This movement may be small and confined to a quick dodge or a step away, or it may be a speed movement for several paces. Basketball is a game of cutting and dodging movements and actions like this are necessary all the time.

BASKETBALL HABITS

With beginners there should always be regular practice in certain definite underlying sections of play. Young players must quickly acquire a good basketball stance which they can assume at the end of a fast run and maintain when they are in a position of defence whether they are moving forwards, backwards or sideways. They must learn to jump high, retain balance in the jump, and subsequently land in a position of balance; this is essential for so much of their work consists of jumping to shoot and offensive and defensive rebounding. They must learn to pivot using either foot, and their pivot turns must be done at speed whether the player has the ball or is dodging an opponent. To help in these aspects the coach will work the group as a unit. He will demand movement forwards, sideways or backwards, quick stops and turns followed by immediate further movement. The idea is not to rush the players from place to place but to train them in the basic habits of basketball. A basketball player does not move about the court as a soccer player does on the football pitch. The approach to basketball is very different and the coach who ignores this specialized movement produces only a half-rate team.

2. Speed start and speed stop

This running, jumping, stopping and pivoting imposes a considerable strain on leg and foot muscles, and regular practice will make for a marked increase in strength. Basketball also calls for strong arms capable of speeding a ball over considerable distance or having power in hand so that shots can be taken easily. The action of passing is not sufficiently robust to develop great strength so the training of beginners should include exercises to remedy this. There can be simple activities like double arm punching forwards or more strenuous ones like arm bending from front support, chinning the beam or exercises with weights. Arm strengthening exercises are most important and are often sadly neglected. The adverse results of this neglect are that players fail through sheer lack of strength to acquire certain skills within a reasonable period of practice.

THE BASKETBALL COACH

BASKETBALL TESTS

The youngster, trained and coached through the whole range of fundamentals and made aware of patterns of play, is excellent material for development to high standards. He should be confident in his ability, for the whole of his preparation will have been in the nature of a combined effort between himself and his coach and this relationship breeds confidence. To ensure that he will achieve a high standard in all the fundamentals, the coach must impose some form of testing during the preparatory lessons. These tests are not difficult to devise and the coach can easily make up a useful battery of tests covering shooting, rebounding, dribbling, passing and guarding. There should be several tests for each fundamental and one part at least must include working against opposition. In this way the dribbling test could be in three sections:

(*a*) Speed dribbling covering a half-court distance,

(*b*) Protective dribbling, where an attacker is close marking and the dribbler is moving around merely retaining possession of the ball,

(*c*) Attacking dribbling, as in a 'one on one' situation, where the attacker is trying to break past a marking opponent.

As a result of these tests, the coach will give a percentage mark or an assessment on a three grade system of good, average or weak to each player, and the markings should be openly displayed on the club notice-board. This will allow the players to review their progress and should encourage them to work to eradicate weaknesses. The tests should also provide an incentive for the players of average ability to pit their skill against the good players, for obviously if they can beat such opponents then they will have improved their own grading. The good players are also on their mettle for in such practices they have their own high standing to maintain.

TRAINING SESSIONS

On all occasions during training practices the coach must set an example of efficiency and pleasant personality. He must always be punctual and must insist that his players are punctual too. His kit should be neat and tidy and his personality must dominate the whole occasion. This does not mean that his attitude is that of a dictator but it must be such that every player feels that he is being watched, corrected and encouraged. It is the right of every player to have the impression that he is the most important man on the court and the coach must be aware of this. Training sessions if properly organized and conducted will give pleasure in play and satisfaction in achievement. These two points should be the keynotes of practice.

With more adult players there must still be regular practice, for it is wrong policy to overload a team with so many games that training sessions become an impossibility. One match each week is adequate and this coupled with a training session allows a team to make steady improvement during the course of a season. These two weekly meetings of the club give the contrast in basketball which players need, for on the one hand there is the excitement and nervous tension of competition and on the other the satisfaction and hard work of training. The training session, although conducted to a definite programme, will be to an extent lighthearted and will enable a full development of friendship and club spirit to occur. The good-natured banter between players in the changing room is important and should be encouraged, for the teams are obviously groups of good friends. It is a wise plan for the coach to leave time for the players to get together in the local restaurant or coffee bar when training is over. A session is often spoiled if players have to rush away immediately afterwards and this may occur if there is a late finish on all occasions. The coach can learn a great deal about his players in these informal chats and he can moreover further establish the good relation between player and coach on such occasions as these. All players appreciate the well-organized and well-conducted practice session, they learn to respect the efficiency of the coach in the competition of a hard-fought game, but they also have a genuine desire for the closer friendship which thrives in an atmosphere when they are happy and satisfied with their efforts and are relaxing at their ease. The coffee bar or restaurant sessions are ideal places for the further development of friendship.

THE BASKETBALL COACH

BASKETBALL FITNESS

In pre-season training, and throughout the whole of the season as well, the coach will have the important factor of the fitness of his players uppermost in his mind. Fitness, however, can become a fetish or an endless source of worry: it is something which the unkind and uneducated spectator criticizes so easily. 'They are not fit' is one of those clichés that comes up time after time and all too often it is said without understanding. Obviously the coach must spend time on improving or maintaining the fitness of his players but he must be quite firm and quite settled in his own mind regarding the necessary standard of fitness and the way to obtain it. Fitness is merely one aspect of the game. There are very many others and the over-emphasis of any one of these throughout the whole of a season will make for an unbalanced and possibly a weaker team. Obviously the good basketball player must be fit or he will soon lose the sharp edge of his ability and be useless after a very few minutes of play in a hard-fought game. The coach should never include a player in the team who is obviously unfit, for not only is he a liability but at the same time he is an upsetting influence to the other men who are the whole time doing extra work to cover up his deficiencies.

It must be understood, however, that the fitness training is specific; it is fitness training for basketball. There is a difference between this specific fitness and the fitness required by a soccer player or a swimmer; and although it is true that there is a type of basic fitness, it is fitness only of a moderate degree and should serve as a foundation upon which specific fitness can be built. There are, of course, varied opinions about fitness training and certain continental coaches believe that after the summer lay off, the first part of the training should be aimed at establishing a high degree of personal fitness. This training consists of work with weights, running and speed running and a whole series of bodily exercises aimed to train a man to a high degree of physical perfection. When the players are at this peak of condition, practice and training in basketball is begun. This approach should find little favour with the British coach for not only has he scant time for such training but also he most probably has little conviction that this work has much value. Nevertheless, his players must be fit and fitness training must figure as a definite part of practice sessions.

There is no need, however, for fitness training to be completely divorced from skill training and a happy arrangement can be made whereby skill training is done but at the same time fitness is emphasized. Working in this way, the first part of any training session can be devoted to hard repetitive effort on strenuous practices, and a definite schedule of work for each team member or each small group can be prepared. This type of work, done at full speed and for a period of time that makes for sustained effort will develop endurance and fitness but will also serve to improve skill in the aspects practised.

There are many exercises which lend themselves to fitness training of this sort and basically they are speed movements, with or without the ball, performed either from a position of attack or defence. In this category come speed dribbling up and down the court with quick stops, pivots and turns at varied intervals. Another general exercise can be worked from a two on one situation with the two attackers making quick passes as they speed down the court whilst the defender attempts to position himself for interception. Shooting can also be done with the player making a speed dribble from half court and finishing with a lay-up shot or a jump shot. Countless other exercises can be devised all of which demand full effort from a physical point of view but include basketball skills and definite game aspects. To emphasize the fitness training of the exercises, the coach must prescribe a set number of repetitions for each activity and he must see that each player honours this number. From the examples given above he might decide that the quota for each of his team is ten double trips up and down the court for the individual dribble, ten double trips for the two on one situation and twenty half court dribbles and shots. Movement from one activity to another should be done without rest and the total number of exercises devised by the coach should be developed until it lasts at least half an hour. As the fitness of the team increases, further exercises can be added, or a greater number of repetitions demanded. In this way the fitness work can keep up with the improvement shown by the player. The work can also be regulated to the varied degree of fitness of each player, so one individual may have eighteen repetitions whilst another has considerably more. The aim is to give the right amount to extend each player to the full.

Within the framework of each exercise, the coach should allow the players to use their own individuality. Consequently, in the two on one drill, no one trip along the court will be exactly the same as any other, for on each occasion a different situation will arise according to the disposition of the defender. The attackers must play the situation as they see it and learn to react at speed in the right way. Herein lies skill training as well as fitness training, and the players will learn from these patterns how to deal with similar situations which occur during a game.

In selecting the fitness exercises, the coach will have in mind the main movements of basketball, which are running, jumping, turning and stopping. In addition, the coach should include exercises which tend to develop the strength of finger, wrist, arm and shoulder muscles. If the coach decides that his team as a whole are weak in a particular aspect, then certain exercises only may be done in order that the weaknesses may be eradicated. An example of this may be a whole series of jumping drills to improve rebounding and jump shooting.

During the period of the fitness training the coach should be moving around amongst the groups and should be keenly observant of their activity but he should adopt the role of a spectator rather than anything else. He will note the tenacity of purpose shown by his players and the true spirit of the athlete in the fight for skill against increasing fatigue. Degrees of fitness will also be obvious for the supremely fit men will be capable of regular increases in repetitions.

After the fitness training the coach will allow the players to cool down for a few minutes by easy jogging around the court; subsequently there should be a definite period of complete relaxation. This can last for about ten minutes during which time the coach can talk on the actual skill training he has in mind for the next part of the practice session. A player who is fit will quickly recover from the arduous work he has just done and the relaxation will put him in the right mood for the next dose of work. There are many coaches who believe that the correct position for relaxation of this sort is to lie on the back with the legs supported at a higher level than the body. It is certainly true that this position conveys a feeling of great ease to many athletes, and as such it is to be recommended.

PROGRAMME PLANNING

In planning his programme, the coach will have in mind the needs of pre-season training, early-season training and mid-season training. His work will vary in early training sessions according to the requirements of the team, hence aspects of fitness, fundamentals, and methods of attack or defence may in turn be emphasized. The aim should be, however, to establish quickly a team of all-round ability and once this has been done, the approach to training should be towards general improvement. Even with the best training, however, teams will show varied degrees of form in each *aspect* of basketball at every match. This may be due to a particular style of play adopted by the opposition or to a temporary loss of form. The coach must not react wildly to this and place a wrong emphasis in training in subsequent practices. Regular coaching according to a well-judged programme is the best method of developing a first-rate team.

GENERAL INFORMATION

Because each practice session and each game is a strenuous affair the coach must include as part of his work some general information about nutrition, hygiene and physical recovery after games. These subjects are very important and all too often they are neglected since the coach finds his time fully occupied in the training itself and in coaching during games. It is an unwise policy, however, to produce a player who shows considerable skill and yet who can never give of his best because he is hampered by a small degree of ill health. Fitness and health do not automatically go hand in hand and the coach must take some precautions to ensure good health.

THE BASKETBALL COACH

Basketball is a hard game demanding a great deal of energy, all of which must be replaced by food. Players will be guided regarding quantity of food by their own appetites but they should also see that their diets are reasonably balanced. This is a sphere in which the coach can only make suggestions but he should definitely give straightforward advice about eating before play or practice. No player should have a substantial meal within three hours of active basketball, and as far as possible, this point should be enforced. This does not mean that players cannot have a light snack before a game, but it should be at least an hour before actual play. There should also be a strict limit on the amount of liquid drunk with this snack meal and this should never be more than one-third of a pint; the liquid should be taken slowly. It is equally wrong as a regular habit to partake of a big meal soon after a strenuous game. The body takes some time for complete recovery following all-out effort and the digestion of a large quantity of food will impose a considerable strain. There are occasions, of course, when an important game is followed by a banquet, and it would be discourteous to refuse such hospitality. Such meals should be the exception and not the general rule.

However fit a player may be it will take him several hours to recover completely after a championship game or a series of games played during a short space of time. Again the coach must be helpful in this situation and he must give wise advice to expedite this recovery phase. Recovery is helped first of all by a warm bath, or preferably a shower. This, followed by a good rub down, gives a feeling of well-being. The shower itself is, however, not enough and the coach should recommend that his players take warm drinks soon after the game and have nine to ten hours of deep sleep during that night. Unless it is necessary, vigorous activity should be avoided the following day and a more than usual supply of liquid should be taken together with doses of liquid glucose. This latter will help the body to return more quickly to its normal state. Advice of this type will be of considerable help to the players and the benefits which are obviously derived will help to establish good habits of health. It would be wrong for the coach to assume the role of a doctor, but he should know the usual state of health of each player and be cautious if he sees a variation from the normal condition. Regular weighing will give some idea of a fall off in health and particular attention should be paid to the player who begins to lose weight. If a weighing scale is left in the changing room the players will make frequent use of it and weight checks will be easy.

The coach should see that minor cuts and bruises received during play are properly treated. Major accidents call for hospital treatment and this obviously must be obtained with all possible speed, but first-aid for the smaller affairs is equally important. Cuts and floor burns can quickly become septic if first-aid is not applied. The first-aid box should always be to hand both during practice and during games, and the contents should consist at least of elastoplast, pads of cotton wool, liquid antiseptic, a preparation for the treatment of athletes' foot, aspirin, tweezers and scissors.

COACHING IN THE GAME

Little has been said of the attitude of the coach as he controls his team from the bench during any major game. He most certainly has an important part to play and it is advisable for him to have some definite plan in mind concerning the use of time-out periods and the interval. Unless this is so, his approach to coaching in the game may be haphazard and only partly effective. In a normal game a time-out may be called after about seven or eight minutes' play and the coach will use this to resolve some of the following points:

1. Who can usually beat his man?
2. Who is experiencing difficulty in holding his man?
3. Are we controlling both offensive and defensive backboards?
4. Are we getting back on defence sufficiently quickly?
5. What have been our most effective methods of attack?
6. Are there any star opponents who should be two-teamed?
7. What are our opponents' main systems of attack and defence?

These are too many questions to put to the team during the one minute of the first time-out, but the chances are that only some of them apply and these should then be discussed. In a later time-out during the first half the coach may instruct his players to try out a particular method of attack just once only. This is to see if the attack bamboozles the defence and if this is so, this move may be reserved for use during a later and more critical stage of the game.

By half time, the coach should know who are his faster men, who are his best rebounders and who are his best shooters. He should also have ascertained his most effective method of attack and defence. Working on this knowledge the tactics for the second half are decided bearing in mind, of course, that the opponents are doing exactly the same thing. The second half may be a time to exploit shock tactics but this is entirely dependent on the run of play. It is the good coach, however, who always has something in reserve to worry his opponents.

Mention has been made earlier of the high importance of the personality of the coach. It is the coach who can contribute considerably to the general enjoyment of the game and he must always be aware of this. For the most part he is dealing with a bunch of teenagers who are full of spirit and life. The determination to enjoy themselves is overriding, but they will take hard work in terrific quantities if it is put over in an objective and pleasurable way. This is the duty of the efficient coach. His pleasure comes from the lively companionship of young people, his pride in the formation of an efficient team, and his satisfaction with the part he has played in the development of youngsters into fine citizens.

2

CLUB ORGANIZATION
AND TEAM DEVELOPMENT

by H. ERRINGTON

Basketball was fostered in England by the Y.M.C.A. and it is
greatly to the credit of this association that interest in the game
was sustained and developed. The early years were full of difficulties for the outlook on games at that period was conservative and
there was a tendency to view with some suspicion any possible
incursion on the popularity of the accepted games of cricket,
football and rugby. There was a real need, however, for an inter-
nationally accepted indoor game. Basketball filled that need and
began to develop in the services, in clubs and in schools. The enthusiasm of physical education teachers was such that Old Boys'
teams were formed either separately or in association with evening
institute classes. Such classes operated to an extent in isolation and
at first there was little competition between group and group. As
the various coaches got together, friendly games were arranged
and it is but a short step from here to organized competition.

FORMING THE NEW CLUB

In this haphazard way, basketball started, and since then, progress has been such that there are now more potential players than
coaches. There is obviously a need for the formation of new clubs
and this calls for accommodation, personnel and organizers. To
ensure a greater degree of success in the early days of club development, two keen and enthusiastic workers are needed; one will be

31

the organizing secretary and the other will undertake the duties of coach. The formation of a club is usually too much work for one man. The immediate objectives of the coach and secretary are to obtain a nucleus of enthusiastic players and to acquire accommodation—and with regard to the latter aspect, the Local Education Authority or the Local Authority are far more prepared to help than is supposed. When a sufficient number of players has been assembled, the group can usually start working under the auspices of the local evening institute. In each area a particular officer, called the Youth Organizer, exists to foster schemes such as these. He will applaud and encourage to the full any initiative of this type which is backed by enthusiasm and common sense. There are certain demands, of course, and these usually consist of getting together a minimum number of players—fifteen is frequently the number—and accepting some adult responsibility, before an Authority will allow the local school to be used. There are certain right and proper formalities regarding the use of public buildings but these formalities are usually wise regulations rather than obstacles.

There are other possibilities for accommodation and these include Territorial Army drill halls and hard-surface playgrounds or playing surfaces. It may be that such areas are not equipped for basketball, and if this applies, the initiative and good faith of the group are shown by their desire and zeal to obtain or make the necessary equipment. When the group is beginning to make satisfactory progress, it is a good idea to give some publicity to the scheme in the local press. There are quite often people living in the area who would be prepared to offer help, or there may be 'foreigners' with basketball experience, living locally, who would become most valuable assets to the team. Within the latter category come a large number of students who would welcome the companionship and enjoyment of a basketball team and would in turn give a great deal of help regarding coaching and playing.

DEVELOPING THE CLUB

The club must try to enrol other people besides actual players for there is an urgent need for non-playing members. Ex-players, parents and even girl friends can be enrolled in this category and all can be found jobs in the general work of organizing, officiating, scoring and timekeeping. Scorers and timekeepers hold important jobs, and there is no reason why these jobs should not be done by women, in fact it is becoming accepted on the Continent that women can act as table officials at international games.

As the team develops, the non-playing members can form the nucleus of a supporters' club, and even if this is only small, it is a well worth-while section of the club. The supporters will no doubt organize a social side to the club and it could possibly be their responsibility to arrange dances and outings, raffles and draws, all of which would help the prestige of the club and the financial status. The team itself will need track suits and kit and perhaps help regarding travelling expenses to distant games; financial subsidies from the supporters' club would assist the full development of an energetic and ambitious team.

PROGRAMME PLANNING

The main objective of the coach is, of course, the development of the playing skill of the team and here the coach is continually fighting against a lack of time. Many club players have other evening class commitments and although an ideal situation would be a training period and a game each week, this is frequently not possible. Coaching is often reduced to a series of practise evenings before the season begins and then occasional practices and some pre-game practice when matches are regular. Every minute on court is precious and none must be wasted. The coach must therefore prepare a carefully worked out training programme before the start of the season; this programme should be posted upon the club notice-board and all team members made fully aware of the contents. The daily programme should be detailed on a blackboard in the gymnasium and this, of course, will be an extract from the complete programme. By working according to a set plan, all aspects will be covered and players will be able to begin practice as soon as they enter the gym. Moreover, the team will know just what to do if the coach is absent; continuity of training can be ensured.

VISUAL AIDS

At the beginning of the season the coach should try to obtain for interest purposes and for demonstration utility, the use of a basketball coaching film. Such films underline the importance of fundamentals and show the correct method of instruction. They also provide a standard of play which the team should try to imitate. The films should never be shown for the purpose of entertainment but should be screened several times during a particular evening. After the first showing, the sound track should be turned down so that the coach can give his own commentary. In this way, the essential facts of each movement can be pin-pointed and a complete explanation made of the successful attempts on the basket, and the reasons for particular weaknesses in defence. If films cannot be obtained, then the team as a whole should be taken to see a game or a training practice of the nearest high-standard team. Again, the essence of the visit is not for interest but rather to analyse and criticize the play.

THE PRACTICE SESSION

The training schedule should be arranged to cover both team work and individual coaching and the coach should be quickly aware of any players who experience difficulties with fundamentals or team movements. Such players should be encouraged to come early to training sessions so that personal help can be given. The greater part of the training should be based on man-to-man play—one attacker against one defender—and coaches should be prepared to spend long periods in this way. Many aspects of the game can be practised by using this method, and these include pivoting, feinting and faking, shooting and dribbling as well as the essential points of defence. A defender skilled in man-to-man play will quickly learn the system of zone defence, but the opposite is not true.

Throughout all practice sessions, the aim of the coach should be to produce progressive activity amongst his players. The basketball court is no place for long discussion and the coach should be brief and precise in his explanations so that practical work can follow quickly. Drills should be chosen with great care, and essentially they should be of the 'short and snappy' type, done at speed and with enjoyment. Dribbling skill can be learned through relay races which are both stimulating and allow for the development of competitive spirit, and training involving medicine balls is helpful if players appear to be lacking in arm or wrist strength. Even more strenuous work can be done in this sphere if small practice Athletic shots are used. These weigh 4–5 lb. and consist of lead shot in a leather case. They have been used with great success by certain continental coaches for training in jump shooting. Players go through the whole movement of the jump shot and attempt to flick the 'practice shot' over a rope which is raised higher and higher as ability improves.

3. Jump shot

A large proportion of practice time should be devoted to shooting, and here success rather than style is the yardstick. Unorthodox shooting does not matter so long as good results are obtained, but the coach will be advised not to tolerate any deviation from the fundamental principles of shooting if players are getting poor results. Part of the shooting practice will include 'free shooting' and work in this aspect of the game is a 'must' for all players. Too many games are lost as a result of poor free shooting for which there is no excuse at all. The easiest free shot to perform is the two-handed underarm action from which the ball is easily 'swung' into the basket. It might be a good policy for the coach to insist that all players adopt this simple style for free shots.

During the practice sessions, the coach will teach some set moves but these should be small in number and essentially simple to operate. There are certain periods during a game when moves can easily be made and the best examples are from a jump ball, an out of bounds play and a free throw. A further set play should be practised for a fast break situation. Regular work done on all these movements will certainly pay good dividends and may account for 20 points in a game. As a definite part of the training, the coach should see that his players have a thorough understanding of the rules, and a sufficient knowledge of officiating technique to allow them to take the whistle during practice scrimmages. These scrimmages should be cut down to a minimum of time but should be hard fought and efficiently refereed. *Free scrimmages should never be a major part of any training session.*

PRE-GAME AND POST-GAME TACTICAL DISCUSSIONS

American coaches make quite a feature of obtaining advance information about the teams they are due to meet in league games and competitions. This 'scouting' of opponents, as it is known, can be of considerable help and it is possibly one of the duties which could be undertaken by a member of the supporters' club. Obviously the coach must give direction to the scout to help him assess the play of a particular team but the report required need not be complicated. A simple report may merely answer such questions as, 'Who are the chief scorers?' 'What type of shots do they use?' 'Whereabouts on court are they when they shoot?' etc. As scouts show degrees of improvement they will be able to isolate the weaknesses and strong points of players in these rival teams and subsequently make a report on them. It is most helpful for the coach to know in advance that a particular opponent has a very accurate set shot but does not like to be crowded or that someone else is an extremely good cutter and always veers off to his right. Armed with such facts, the coach can forewarn his players and prepare them to look out for these habits of play right from the start of the game.

It may be regarded as bad policy for the coach to say overmuch to his team during the last few minutes before a game commences. The team has been drilled and trained and the players must be allowed to play their ordinary game. If it is an away match, the coach should draw attention to any peculiarities about the court and he should compare the state of the floor and the liveliness or otherwise of the backboards with those of the home court. He should also impress his players not to be put off their game by the officials' decisions but to accept them in a calm manner. His final words will be to boost the confidence of his players and to encourage them to give of their utmost. From an atmosphere such as this, the players should go out, keyed up and determined to win.

COACHING IN THE GAME

During the actual match, the coach should sit with his substitutes so that they will be aware of his 'reading' of the game and will know just what to do before they take their place on court. The coach should train his substitutes when going on court, to shake hands with the players they are replacing. This represents an exchange of confidence and also provides an opportunity for the two players to check their particular opponent. An omission or a mistake on this occasion can lead to the opposing side making quick baskets and possibly to the coach using up a valuable 'time-out' to rectify this simple fault.

When the coach calls a 'time-out' he must see that the whole minute is entirely at his disposal. He should not tolerate interruptions by any players for these will completely spoil the review of the game which he intends to give to his team. This review should be both general and personal. The general assessment will help all the players to understand much better the strategy and tactics of the opponents, and from this basis of knowledge, particular remarks can be made about the weakness and strong points of individual players in the opposition. During the course of the game the rival team will make changes in play which the coach must quickly recognize and he will use further time-outs to pass this information on. Before the interval, the coach should have formed an accurate assessment of play and he should have prepared his team for the majority of eventualities.

It is often the policy of a coach to allow his first five to settle down on court and play unchanged during the first ten minutes. Where this applies, the coach is advised to send two or three immediate substitutes away from the court area for a short period so that they can continue to 'warm up'. Players who are on the bench for several minutes soon find that muscles begin to stiffen up and accuracy of touch is for the moment lost. It is wrong for players to go on court in this condition for as soon as a substitute becomes a player he must immediately be able to work his full capacity.

ANALYSIS CHARTS

As we have seen, it is the duty of the coach to make general assessments of the play throughout the changing phases of the game. It is impossible, however, for him to remember detail, so to help him in this matter he should appoint a member from his supporters' club to assist him with game analysis. The simplest analysis consists of recording every shot taken, noting the position from which the shot was attempted and 'ringing' the successful shots. For this the recorder will need an outline plan of the court and a pencil. Whenever a shot is made, the number of the player will be entered on the plan at the approximate shooting position and a circle drawn round the number if the shot scores. From the plan the coach can easily see both the shooting form of his players and the range of shooting. Record cards can obviously be more complicated and can analyse whatever factors the coach chooses. They can show such things as loss of ball, interceptions, defensive and offensive rebounding and even general participation in the game. An analysis of this latter aspect would need five recorders, with each recorder watching a particular player and noting the number of times he is in contact with the ball and the number of runs he makes to open positions. The individual analysis regarding ball handling would be split into passing, dribbling, beating a man, rebounding, shooting and intercepting. From the total analysis and working to a time factor basis the coach could establish how the general work of the team was shared out amongst the players. As a result he would have direct evidence to show that certain players were much more hardworking than others and this should help to level out game participation by each player in subsequent matches. Major analyses of this sort cannot be used by the coach during the course of a game but they would be essentially valuable in mid-week training sessions when the general development of the team is being reviewed.

AFTER THE GAME

Immediately a game is over, the coach should make it his duty to mingle with his players whilst they are changing. This should be an occasion of congratulation to those who have done particularly well and quiet praise to the others. The coach should take the attitude that all his team have striven to do as well as they possibly can and obviously there should be no recriminations for such efforts. If there is time after changing, the team should get together with the coach over a cup of tea. The coach can then 'tell the story of the match' explaining methods of play used by both teams and reviewing the degrees of success. During this talk, individual opinions from the players should be sought but nothing should be allowed to spoil the atmosphere of happiness and enjoyment that the coach takes it upon himself to create.

THE PLAYER COACH

The ideal coach to a basketball team should have had, amongst other things, considerable playing experience, and a more than average ability as a player. If, during his playing days he has been a member of an area team or better, and has had an opportunity of taking part in games against continental sides, he should stand every chance of achieving success as a coach. Obviously the man who has been a regular member of the national team and has participated in the European Games and pre-Olympic tournaments should be admirably fitted to become an excellent coach. Such a player is steeped in basketball knowledge, his playing ability will be a real inspiration to a team which comes under his charge, and he should be keen and willing to pass on his knowledge and enjoyment to groups of youngsters. He should become acquainted with the examinations drawn up by the A.B.B.A. and not feel too important to take these examinations. It may be that he sees shortcomings in these examinations but he will do a great service to basketball by sitting for the examination and subsequently by attempting to improve them. The examinations demand a good knowledge of basketball, and an ability to coach the game; so no player should take it for granted that because he is a good exponent, he is automatically a good coach. His ambition should be to sit for the National Grade Examination for this will give him the highest standing. Coupled with this he should attempt the Area Grade Officiating Award since his coaching ability is dependent upon a sound knowledge of the rules and an understanding of the viewpoint of the referee.

A person with such qualifications should prove an excellent coach for he has everything that the position demands. He has the knowledge to explain all the theoretical problems that will come up in game discussions and moreover he has the ability to demonstrate correctly all the fundamentals and plays of the game itself. He can draw on his experience to teach set moves and their various options, and he can show where each move is likely to break down.

THE CHANGE-OVER: PLAYER-COACH TO COACH

When a player of good calibre becomes a coach to a junior team he can do considerable service initially by playing and coaching as well. His play will help to establish the team in the league and possibly do a great deal towards winning promotion to a higher league. The successful team attracts players of good potential and in this way the club will be built up to a strength that a second team can be formed. The duties of the coach are now doubled and a big decision begins to shape up before him. This concerns stopping regular play with the main team and becoming, as it were, a full-time coach to both teams. The decision is hard to make, however, for it is very enjoyable to continue playing. There is considerably more behind the change-over, for this may mark the end of a particular phase in life when youthful effervescence is beginning to fade and perhaps a certain degree of leg weariness, never experienced before, is beginning to show itself after a heavy session. This change is bound to come, it is quite natural and it applies to everyone. It is far better to take it at the right time when the decision can happily be made by the player and actually regretted by the team rather than forced on the player by the team itself. Moreover, coaching is a most enjoyable and worth-while job bringing rewards that are just as satisfying as playing.

Needless to say, many player-coaches defer this change-over phase and the reactions on the club are usually unsatisfactory. The player-coach is doing two jobs, neither of which he can perform efficiently. Whilst he is on court he is probably worrying about substitutes and time-outs and this makes for bad play from his own side. When he is on the bench he may be considering that he could do the job of the players on court much better and this leads to dissatisfaction. The player-coach must know when to pull out of the game and on this matter an early decision is better than a late one.

The Amateur Basketball Association working in co-operation with the Central Council of Physical Recreation seeks to help players become player-coaches and finally coaches. Courses are regularly organized throughout the country to do just this job. Many existing basketball clubs would welcome a person of this calibre with open arms and the service such players could do towards improving the standard of the game would be of greatest value. Lowly placed clubs are often in this position because they depend for development on the limited knowledge of inexperienced men. As a result, many clubs in this category play basketball as a recreational activity rather than as an enjoyable, vigorous and skilful game. The proper progression of these teams and other similar teams can only come from within basketball itself and this means the development of good players through the stages player-coach to coach.

CLUB ORGANIZATION

The basketball season, extending from October to May, is a long and strenuous affair and for very many teams the busiest time is towards the end of the season. In spite of this, the club usually wishes to keep together during the summer. When this applies, the coach should consider several different aspects for this period of time. First of all he must ease up the intensity of work or the players will become stale and jaded, resulting in an off-form approach to the next season.

One very easy and simple change is to play the summer games outside and this has many advantages. Playing in the fresh air is quite a tonic and if a proper approach is made, courts are not difficult to obtain. Local authorities are very co-operative in allowing basketball teams to use the hard surfaces of public tennis courts or netball pitches for organized games, although, of course, the club itself may have to provide the necessary equipment.

Another advantage of outdoor courts is that the game is taken to the public. It is surprising how many people during pleasant evenings will stop to watch any organized activity. Well-played games will turn this casual audience into regular attenders, especially if some publicity is provided and certain information about the game is given. Local authorities are anxious for people to make use of parks and open spaces, and the sight of a large audience watching two well-matched sides will encourage councillors to make better provision for future games. Some publicity about future games can be obtained through the local press and regular inserts about these fixtures should ensure a good attendance. Basketball is too much of a concealed sport and an unknown quantity in England but if an appreciative audience can be encouraged to watch outdoor games then it is very possible that a proportion of these people will come to see the indoor winter games during the season itself. Information should be available at the outdoor court giving details of the centre used by the club during the winter, the league in which the team plays and the nights of the week when matches are usually arranged. It is quite possible that this publicity will attract players or other people with basketball experience who would be great assets to the club on the management or on the officiating side.

OUTDOOR BASKETBALL

The propaganda value of outdoor basketball is enormous; in fact if the game is treated as an outdoor activity it may develop more quickly.

There is no need for these outdoor matches to be merely straight games between two clubs, for it is not a difficult matter to organize rallies where teams play for short periods on an American tournament basis. Such rallies can include school teams, junior teams and senior teams. The teams will play in separate pools, but the occasion will provide an opportunity for players of the lower ages to see good-class basketball.

The coach should also make his team available for demonstrating games at fêtes and other open-air functions. This again can be most enjoyable to the team and should prove to be of good propaganda value. It is not enough, however, simply to go along and play, for the occasion must be properly staged. There should be a public address system and someone detailed to act as announcer and commentator. In this way, the teams can be properly introduced and star players or local players mentioned. Certain explanations can be given about the game and the score can be noted after each basket. The game itself should not be of long duration and twenty minutes is probably quite enough. Stoppages should be reduced to a minimum and the interval should be completely cut out. It is of great importance that both teams should be well dressed and well behaved on these occasions. Finance enters into these demonstration games and if a team can put over an exciting and interesting spectacle the coach should be prepared to ask for a donation of at least £5 towards club funds.

It may be argued that British weather is not conducive to outdoor basketball, but our climate is little different from that of Belgium and northern France, and in these parts outdoor basketball flourishes. Quite a feature of northern France is the number of basketball courts set up in the market places and car parks.

CLUB ORGANIZATION

These areas are natural gathering places for people and consequently basketball games are well supported. In Belgium there are far fewer indoor courts than there are in England but the game thrives on outdoor courts. Belgium has 20,000 registered players, which is a fantastic number for such a small country, and the game of basketball rates third in popularity, coming after football and professional cycling. Here is an example of development that coaches in England should be prepared to follow, and league management committees should terminate the winter season in April and organize summer outdoor leagues.

CONTINENTAL TOURS

As soon as a team has reached a reasonable standing and has been playing together as a unit for three or four season, the coach and management of the club should consider the organization of a basketball tour. Such tours are not difficult to arrange, involving merely the usual holiday details together with the addition of two or three basketball games during the period of time. Obviously, the coach will choose opponents who are of the same calibre as his own team otherwise the games played on the tour will be of small interest. It is also unwise to travel a long distance for a single game or to make the holiday so rushed that there is no opportunity for free time and enjoyment in the area that is being visited.

Suitable occasions for such tours are the Easter and Spring holiday weekends and, of course, the summer holiday. During the long weekends, travel can be done on the Friday evening and games played on the Saturday and Sunday. The most convenient form of travel is by mini-bus and these 12–14 seaters are neither expensive to hire nor difficult to drive or park.

The tour *par excellence* is, of course, the continental tour. This can be both an exciting holiday and a wonderful opportunity to meet new clubs and to see different conditions and styles of play. For clubs in the southern part of England it is no great distance to the French and Belgian coasts and the ports of Harwich, Dover, Folkestone, Newhaven and Southampton provide regular and reasonably inexpensive passages to continental areas where basketball flourishes. There are basketball leagues based around Ostend, Calais, Boulogne, Dieppe and Le Havre and each of these particular townships could form a centre in which the two or three games of the tour could be played. Moreover, they are all seaside towns and are very pleasant places; the people are accustomed to English visitors and are usually very pleased to make them welcome. There is no difficulty regarding language for a great many people on the Channel coast speak a smattering of English. The more adventurous clubs may go beyond the coastal area and should they wish to do so they will find excellent teams in Brussels and Paris.

To make the preliminary arrangements, the coach or secretary of the club should write to the national organization of the particular country. The addresses are:

1. *France:* Fédération Française de Basketball, 65 Rue de Victorie, Paris IX.

2. *Belgium:* Fédération Royale Belge de Société de Basketball, 27 Avenue P.H. Spaak, Bruxelles 7.

3. *Holland:* Nederlandse Basketball Bond, Overtoom 244, Amsterdam.

In the letter, the coach should give full details of the team and the approximate playing ability. This may present something of a problem. There are in England, however, certain teams well known on the continent—the Polytechnic, and certain clubs in the top section of the National Basketball League, and the Central Y.M.C.A. Using any of these as a standard, the coach can compare his team to the first, second or third team of either of the English clubs, and on this basis suitable clubs will be found. As soon as the games have been confirmed, permission for the tour must be obtained from the National Executive Committee of the A.B.B.A. This permission is rarely refused but the asking of the request is more than a courtesy notice, for the A.B.B.A. would obviously not grant the request if it were not from a group of affiliated players or if it were considered that the team would bring dishonour to the association.

The idea of a continental tour should be talked over by the coach and the club several months before the proposed holiday. From the time of the initial letter to the foreign association it may take three to four months before all arrangements are complete. This period of time is useful, however, for it enables the team to do the required money saving; this can quite often be made through a weekly collection. If travel is to be arranged by public transport, an early booking of tickets is advisable especially for the Easter and Spring holidays. Groups of fifteen can travel at the cheap party rate and with a group of this size another person can go as party leader for a very small additional amount.

It is advisable for the party organizer to draw up an information sheet giving all the necessary details. This will include times of departure, information about stops and changes *en route*, addresses of hotels abroad, lists of articles of clothing required by the players, places of interest to be seen during the trip, and news of the opponents. These sheets should be prepared in sufficient numbers for one copy to be given to each person. Most important —everyone should be reminded about passports.

The first game of the tour should not be played too soon after arrival, for time and opportunity must be allowed for the English team to see and practice on the basketball court. The court surface may consist of asphalt, concrete, paving slabs or shale and the site will be in the open air in any suitable spot in the town.

The game itself will be played as arranged unless the weather conditions are such that play is an impossibility. Wind and light rain does not deter continental players and since foreign teams honour their own fixtures in varied weather, English teams must make the best of things and play too. An extreme example of adverse conditions occurred during the England–Belgium International game at Heyst in 1958. A gale force wind was blowing at the time and the backboards were swaying at least six inches from side to side. It was necessary to allow for the wind before making a shot or a free shot. In spite of these somewhat strange conditions, the continental teams are good, their hospitality is first-rate and the support they receive from their locality is tremendous.

It is most important that the touring side be well turned out and well conducted for the players are ambassadors of English basketball. Rightly or wrongly the standard of basketball in England will be judged by the play and behaviour of a particular team. The team will obviously play to the peak of its ability but it should also strive to convey a good impression by efficiently organizing the warm-up and the final cheer and by being business-like rather than casual in substitutions and time-outs. For the warm-up, the team should come out as a unit and should immediately begin drills or activities in which every player is occupied. The tempo of the warm-up should increase and reach a climax about five minutes before the game is scheduled to begin. A halt is then called and the team is withdrawn from court. It is a custom with continental teams for a formal introduction to be made, and the captains exchange pennants and the players exchange badges. The pennants are not difficult to make, and the materials needed are coloured or white satin, braid, a tassel and the local club or district badge. After cutting to size, the pennant is sewn, overlocked or stuck; the cost is about £1. For the introduction to the game the teams run on court and line up on the free throw line facing each other. Announcements are made, after which the captains exchange pennants and the rest of the teams run across the court and hand badges over to their opposite numbers.

Once a continental tour has been attempted, this item will become a major factor in the club programme. New areas will be visited and new friends will be found and sport will be playing its true part in bringing together in happy relationship people from many parts of the world.

3

BASKETBALL AS A MAIN ACTIVITY
IN SCHOOLS

by A. J. SMITH

Basketball in its earlier days was regarded by certain soccer and rugger teams, and even by physical educationists, as an efficient and strenuous mid-week practice for the Saturday major game. The conditions of the game with its small court area made for an abundance of activity and appeared to speed up player reaction. Moreover, it was presumed that many basketball skills bore a direct relationship to those of the country's major games so on a second count the game became acceptable.

Played in this way, the game was boisterous and rough, in fact a crude expression of the precision and skill that basketball at its best could show. Many teams, however, continued to play in this fashion and developed a degree of ability as a result of regular games. The players in such teams felt no need for a mastery of the fundamentals for they used the game as a conditioner and a recreation. They played with fighting qualities and in a rugged way for these two attributes provided the basis of so much of their work-out on the games field.

During this period of development, basketball was not properly understood and since play was obviously much more enjoyable than practice, club teams and school teams based their work on play. It was found that the game was popular with youngsters and apparently could be readily attempted by the majority of boys. A certain degree of clumsiness in play was accepted for it was a new game, not fully appreciated and not properly officiated, but

48

becoming fashionable in schools. The majority of teachers had had no experience of it in colleges of education, but greatly to their credit, they were enthusiastic and tried to learn quickly. They were urged on by the fact that the boys liked it and wanted to play despite individual shortcomings of physique, intelligence, courage or ball sense. Here was a game that offered proximity to action and to an extent a goodly share of actual play. Moreover, the game consisted of many natural movements in which young-sters rejoiced, and this made for its further popularity.

As the game progressed, correct coaching began to develop and the results were that the secondary schoolboy acquired a high standard of skill and showed himself to be potentially greater than the early international players who had been brought up to a large extent on play experience. There were still weaknesses amongst the schoolboys and many appeared to be directly due to the late introduction of the game during the school life. At first it was pre-sumed that 13 years old was a good age to start, and weight was given to this opinion by the fact that the full-sized basketball was difficult for younger lads to control. It is now accepted that basket-ball should be introduced at a much earlier age. Many of the skills are combinations of jumping, shooting, passing, catching and dribbling, and all of these are athletic and some are definitely gymnastic in their nature. Such skills should be acquired before the youngster has to contend with the accelerated growth period between 13 to 15 years, when neuro-muscular control may be difficult. Ideally, the game should be started in the primary school or certainly during the first year of secondary education. This will ensure that sufficient skill is acquired to make second-year games bear a reasonable resemblance to basketball proper.

TEACHING THE SKILLS

Basketball skills can easily be taught during the normal P.E. lessons and many of the basic movements bear similarity to other facets of physical education. The upward jump made when head-ing a football is in part like the movement made for the jump shot, the drive for a lay-up shot compares with the run up for the high jump; the baseball pass is similar to the javelin throw. New skills,

D   49

therefore, can be introduced as class activities and when some degree of proficiency has been attained they can be included in group work or during the warm-up section.

In the teaching of all physical skills, once the movement has been understood, subsequent emphasis must be on the maximum opportunity for supervised practice. This opens up the major problems of basketballs and baskets. One basketball for each boy is the optimum for the practice of shooting drills and dribbling drills, and one between two for ball passing work. Obviously basketballs cannot be provided in this quantity but the problem can to a large extent be solved by the use of cheap plastic balls. The two main baskets on the courts are insufficient for the amount of shooting practice which every group must have. Shooting and the approach to shooting are of vital importance and extra baskets must be set up. Two training baskets should be installed along each side line, and if these are properly placed, practice games can be played across the court. Small additional baskets which hook on to wall bars or beams are also most useful. The extra fixed baskets will usually be installed by the local education authority or they may be made at school in co-operation with the woodwork and metalwork departments.

TEAM DEVELOPMENT

Where there is adequate equipment and considerable opportunity for practice, basketball has every possibility of becoming a major activity in the school. Under these favourable circumstances, a large body of good basketball players will be produced, all of whom will be ready and eager to fight for positions in the representative sides. Consequently, teams chosen under these circumstances will consist of sound players, skilful in the game and willing to work together as efficient and spirited sides. There will be no room for the temperamental star player who may in some games show brilliance whilst in others ineffectiveness. Moreover, where a basketball interest of this magnitude has been created, there will be an abundance of well-informed spectators ready to support any main game. These enthusiasts should also be given opportunity to play in open competition for under normal circumstances, no boy is prepared to train unless there is some definite objective in view.

BALL HANDLING

Of all the fundamentals of the game, ball handling is the most important during introductory stages, and the correct methods of passing and catching must be practised until they become second nature. When players anticipate receiving a pass, they should be taught to form a 'funnel' with the hands. This will act firstly as a target to the player passing the ball and secondly will serve to cushion the ball so that it is taken quietly and properly. The ball should never be slapped with the palms of the hands and if this action should occur as it may do in early stages, the derisive cry of 'slap' is usually enough to eradicate the weakness.

4a. Finger follow through in shooting

4. Rebound shot

The basic passes need to be taught separately. These include the chest pass, the one-hand push pass, and the baseball pass. Practice repetitions should come in hundreds not in tens, and tests should be devised with rewards for speed and accuracy. During training on all the passes, maximum finger follow through should be continually stressed until it becomes part of each player's habit pattern. Finger follow through is highly important in passing but is vital in shooting, and the early acquisition of this movement is a necessity for any would-be top-class player. The Americans stress this follow through for they have found that in shooting, the more successful players were those who worked in this way. In the action of passing, wrist snap should be emphasized. This will prove to be a difficulty with young players in their early stages of learning but subsequent practice will develop strong supple wrists. One very important result of this development will be that the amount of arm action or 'winding up' as it is sometimes known prior to a chest pass will be reduced to an absolute minimum. Accurate passes can then be snapped away before they can be blocked by opponents. Immediately after the passing action has been completed, the youngsters should be coached to leave their fingers 'out to dry' for this will help to develop complete relaxation.

SHOOTING

Where a particular skill is a combination of several basic movements as in the case of the jump shot or the lay-up shot, it is a good idea for the boys to practise the skill without using the ball. Young players tend to think in terms of the ball and the basket rather than the gymnastic movement which gets them into the position for the shot; consequently they rush the ball away without considering what their body is doing. The technique of the jump shot and the lay-up shot is difficult to acquire and it is only rarely that the action can be successfully taught as a complete movement. A useful introduction to the lay-up shot is to have the boys running round the court, driving in to the basket and jumping to try and touch the net. In this way they will learn to coordinate the correct take-off foot with the shooting hand and they will also establish the correct take-off point for the shot. This method is even more valuable when teaching the left-hand lay-up or when introducing more advanced shots like the turn-around jump shot. Once the technique is efficient, practice can be continued using the ball. The boy already has the feel of the shot and he should practice until he can reproduce the same movement with the ball as he did without it. It is a simple matter to teach large numbers in this way, for the exercise can be treated as a class activity.

BASKETBALL IN SCHOOLS

In early stages, all skills must be kept within the strength and scope of the youngsters, for simple skills well executed will lay the foundations of good basketball; in contrast, a fundamental which has been practised in a faulty way will be very difficult to correct at a later stage. It is with these thoughts in mind that the teacher should select the progressions and weigh the drills carefully. He should also consider adapting the game to the ability of his group. Boys of twelve years old will find that set shots from a range of fifteen feet are difficult to perform; youngsters of this age therefore should be encouraged to use lay-up shots and one-hand push shots instead.

BASKETBALL DRILLS

Football fundamentals together with both good and bad habits of play are learned by either kicking a small ball around in the streets or in countless pick-up games played at odd times. Basketball in this country has no such period of learning. Very often the first time that the boy meets the game is when he moves into his secondary school. At this stage he probably has no basic knowledge of the game so it is quite ridiculous to put ten youngsters on the court and expect them to play. Introductory time must be spent in teaching basic skills and in devising drills which are fitted for the correct practice of the skills. Basketball has as part of its tradition an almost endless variety of drills designed to simulate game conditions and develop certain techniques, or to be used as pre-game warm-up drills. Many of these accepted drills have been devised by American coaches for particular purposes, and it is wrong to take them out of context and use them for our own youngsters without making some slight adaptation. It is essential that all drills should be made objective and possibly competitive, if interest in them is to be maintained. Group can work against group, shooting drills can easily be made competitive, and points can be awarded in passing drills for the greatest number of successful passes.

For a drill to be really good, it needs to be as near to game conditions as possible, and outside elements which are foreign to the normal course of events should not be introduced. Many

53

dribbling drills fail because they are geared to false situations. In this category appear all those drills where a leader, by means of visual signals, directs a dribbler to manœuvre in artificial situations. It is much better for the youngsters to learn dribbling by playing 'dodge and mark' or 'tag'. This will certainly help to develop peripheral vision and will teach the ability to stop and start, and change both speed and direction. Where drills are practised in groups, it follows that the smaller the group the greater is the amount of work done by each player. Relay work involving dribbling down the court and shooting into a far basket or a side basket should be done in pairs. Teams should work from both ends of the court and this general criss-cross movement over the court will certainly help to develop good ball control as well as peripheral vision. In practices of this type it is never enough for a boy just to shoot at the basket, he must stay there until he has scored. Where the technique of the lay-up shot has been mastered, no more than three attempts should be necessary before the shot is made. Again, where youngsters are working freely over the court in a dribbling-shooting drill like the one described, if there are six baskets on the court, three pairs can be assigned to each basket. Thirty-six youngsters are therefore getting considerable practice on a court which is equipped with two main baskets and four subsidiary baskets. It is a good idea also to specify the type of shot required during practices and to have some kind of reward for the first pair and a forfeit for the last.

CONDITIONED GAMES

At all stages in the coaching of basketball, the employment of the conditioned game is most valuable, and with young players, the aspect which should be emphasized is that of non-contact. In the excitement of play, youngsters tend to barge and tackle. This can be prevented to a very large extent by the introduction of a condition whereby any fouling is penalized by the award of a point to the offended team. A useful rule to add at this primary stage is to penalize with a foul any boy who attempts to knock the ball out of an opponent's hands, for this action is a main cause of contact with inexperienced players. The introduction of such a rule gives the player in possession time to decide what to do with the ball before his anticipated move is broken. This does not mean, of course, that the ball holder should stand facing his opponent and remain motionless for he should be coached to pivot and attempt to protect the ball.

Further conditions can be established regarding dribbling. The majority of teams indulge in too much dribbling and this can be curbed by making the dribble a violation. It may seem that a game which is conditioned to protect the ball holder and stop the dribbler must become a slow-passing game. This fault, however, can be eradicated by coaching the youngsters to take full responsibility of playing 'off the ball' and by 'whistling up' players who hold the ball too long.

Players should be encouraged to experiment with a variety of shots during practices and opportunities should be made to try simple plays which have been developed. Left-hand shots, or shots following certain movements, should therefore be scored at three or four points each, and successful shots following blocks or screens can be similarly rewarded. Should a team need practice in a three on two situation they can be made to play against seven men. Two of the seven will always stay in the back court and two will remain in the front court, consequently the handicapped team will always find two opponents waiting for them in a break-away situation.

ASSIGNMENTS

Another useful aid to help youngsters practice is the allocation of assignments. By this method each player is given an individual assignment which consists of a number of passes, followed by repetitions of particular drills in a definitely specified order. The players may either be given a definite number of repetitions to complete, or a specified time in which they aim to do as many repetitions as possible. The actual assignments can be enlarged to include certain aspects of weight training and circuit training but these additions should not be considered until the players have reached a reasonable standard.

BASKETBALL IN SCHOOLS

HABITS OF PLAY

With the introduction of drills and conditioned games, there comes an excellent opportunity to eliminate fundamental errors or unnecessary movement. There are certain habits of play which all boys appear to try and some of them can be disastrous if the practice is allowed to persist. The more common ones are the use of one hand to deflect a pass downwards into a dribble, the excessive 'winding up' that develops before a set shot is taken, the sideways swinging movement that takes place after the ball has been gathered preparatory to a lay-up shot, and the coach's nightmare, which is the single bounce prior to passing or shooting. Some faults are direct results of bad-habit patterns, but others which may be termed gymnastic faults are often due to the incorrect placing of the ball in relation to the body. These result in bad balance and awkward movement. It is possible that some faults are 'nervous' habits partially caused by lack of confidence. The coach will approach the elimination of these bad habits in various ways, using explanation, corrective drills or even dictatorial methods according to the situation.

The development of peripheral vision, ambidextrous shooting, passing and dribbling together with faking and feinting should be encouraged right from the start. These are not just additional facets for the advanced player but are basic fundamentals of the game. Many drills give ample opportunity for the development of split vision; good examples are mass dribbling drills and shooting drills as well as the obvious pepper-potting drills. Shots using the left hand should be taught separately and if practice games are biased in favour of these shots, players will become 'two gun' men. Faking and feinting should follow hard upon the heels of teaching the first shots and passes, and a result will be that skills like the 'up and under' become an optional way of approaching a shot. Each progression should be made carefully and this applies especially to shooting. One-hand push shots and lay-up shots should be taught first and these should be followed by two-hand set shots, jump shots and hook shots. When boys have mastered the smooth movement of the basic shots and can get the ball away in an easy and relaxed fashion, then and not until then should they attempt turn around shots, scoop shots or any more advanced variations of shooting.

BASKETBALL DEFENCE

From my own experience of coaching basketball, it seems preferable to get the game really moving before a definite attempt is made to teach defensive fundamentals. To young boys, a great deal of the appeal in the game lies in the fact that anyone can score and that the scores can be quite high. As soon as a sufficient command of attack has been mastered, however, man to man principles of defence can be introduced. These principles are the basis of game defence and players well grounded in man to man will easily adapt themselves to other forms of defence. The opposite is not usually true. Moreover, the majority of schoolboys are slow to organize zone defences, and one or two men are often left completely alone to deal with a fast breaking attack. From their own side, youngsters tend to prefer man to man defence for there is a much greater appeal in the definite objective of checking a particular player.

Defensive drills are difficult to devise and both the 'dodge and mark' type and the 'pass ball' type fail because neither drill takes into account the all important aspect of position play. When practising defence, two on two drills give a better concept of position placing and game situation, and on a court where there are six baskets, twenty-four boys can be working at full pressure under these conditions of attack and defence. In the early stages, fairly static drills covering stance, position play and blocking out must be practised. Ideally, the best situation is the one on one, for under these conditions many individual faults can be ironed out. In the one on one itself, the attacker should attempt to drive past his opponent or shoot over the top of him, and the defender should match movement for movement and prevent the shooter from making either type of shot. This calls for controlled movement, delicacy of movement and above all, anticipation, for the defender must close in when a shot is imminent. The same attitude regarding marking must persist when the opponent does not possess the ball and the defender must be equally on his mettle to see that there is no break past. Defence of this type can be practised as a class activity with attacker and defender moving across the gymnasium. When the defensive position is understood and appreciated, it can then be put into a conditioned game; any earlier introduction without due practice would only lead to somewhat messy and rough play. As with all fundamentals, progression will be controlled and such special activities as guarding the pivot man and playing defence on particular opponents will not be introduced until later.

VISUAL AIDS

At first glance, there do not seem to be many visual aids immediately available on basketball but a little searching off the beaten track of physical education, and application to organizations like the Central Council of Physical Recreation, the A.B.B.A. and the E.S.B.B.A. can be most helpful. In addition American sports periodicals, American forces journals, and some of the literature produced by both English and American sports firms will provide quite a good and steady supply of still photographs for the notice-board. It should be remembered, however, that still photographs fail to give any idea of the rhythm of the movement and a picture of a jump shot at the point of release may be superb for demonstrating many points but the 'how did he get there' question remains. By far the best medium for teaching the game is the film; a number of useful films are available in this country from some of the sources named above.

The opportunities of seeing really first-class basketball in this country are comparatively few, consequently films of American professional games have a very real place in filling this gap in a young player's experience. Learning the fundamental and then being shown its application in a game is an excellent teaching sequence, but the recognition of the fundamental in a game is an even more important step, and this can be well illustrated by film.

If there are any good senior teams playing in the locality an approach should be made to them regarding demonstration games. This link between school team and club team must be made, for obviously the school, unless an Old Boys' team is contemplated, will provide juniors for the club and the club will become a natural progression, for the better school players. In the early days of this co-operation, there may be some fear that the apparent rougher play of the club will be copied by the school players; if this appears, it should be immediately eliminated.

GAME PARTICIPATION

Above all, of course, there must be maximum opportunity for the boys to practise the skills they have acquired. More accommodation is required than the playing court in the gymnasium and any suitable playground space should be utilized. Outdoor basketball goals can be built quite inexpensively or even bought reasonably cheaply, and if courts are set up and a number of plastic balls are made available, a great deal of practice can be obtained. In some cases boys have even fixed up rings at home and local authorities have co-operated to the extent of erecting goals in public recreation areas.

Once the game begins in earnest, it is a good idea to set the boys thinking about situations as they arise—this is useful from the point of view of the individual, for he can puzzle out what is right or wrong under the particular circumstances, and equally useful from the team aspect where a group of players are involved. For instance, at a jump ball situation, the following questions may be considered:

Are we likely to win the tap? If we are, who receives the ball next and where do we take it from there? If not, what are we doing to meet our opponents' attack?

Again, here is a team attacking and making effective use of a tall rebounder; what can we do to minimize his effect? How do we get inside this tight zone defence?

These tactical problems will help to highlight the use of screens, blocking out and many of the other offensive and defensive measures peculiar to the game.

Basketball is one of the few games that allows for time-outs, when problems of

5. Winning the tap

59

play can be considered. It is important during practice sessions that there should be opportunity to discuss the consequences of various situations, and all the players should be encouraged to have their say for these on-the-spot discussions will help towards a fuller understanding of the game. Opportunity should be made, therefore, to have more than the usual number of time-outs since the discussions are more important than match restrictions.

INTRODUCTORY GAMES

It is essential that the youngsters acquire a certain ability before they play their first game. Amongst the various skills which they should possess at this stage are shooting and passing, and to help in the development of these aspects, certain introductory games may prove useful. Passball is particularly helpful for although it is a game of very few rules it will nevertheless serve to maintain interest and at the same time help to foster good passing skill.

Skittle ball can also be used to advantage and is especially suitable for the small boys who cannot manage shots at the basket. With coaching and experience, the elements of court circulation begin to appear and this has a most useful carry over when the full game of basketball is attempted. It is helpful if a circular zone of 6 ft. radius, from which all players are excluded, is drawn around the skittle, and a table top placed on its side is put behind the skittle. The table top will act as a rebound board and so will give a greater semblance to the major game. During early games, the majority of youngsters take some little time to consider a shooting situation before actually making the shot. If they are heavily blocked by another equally enthusiastic youngster at this stage, the whole object of the game is spoiled. The games, therefore, should be conditioned so that a certain freedom of shooting is allowed and this type of quick blocking does not arise.

The introduction of the American game of 'Biddy Basketball' where all court sizes, height of ring and size of ball are scaled down, is naturally the perfect medium for early basketball. Under these conditions, younger lads will give better performances when they do not have to make such efforts merely to reach the ring.

BASKETBALL IN SCHOOLS

Unfortunately, very few basketball stands in this country are designed so that the height can be adjusted and very often the use of a lighter and smaller ball is the only possible modification. Most English indoor courts are smaller than the international senior standards and from this point of view there is little worry of youngsters having to run too far.

The School Team

The selection of players for the school team brings with it many problems, particularly in a school where other major sports have to be taken into consideration. It is, however, only on the rare occasion, from my own experience, that trial games to determine the team are necessary, since outstanding players are noticed and groomed as they move up through the school. This method of selection is by far the best for choosing the team.

The success of any basketball team depends to a very large extent on the ability of the players to move the ball quickly and to move it with a constructive purpose in mind. For these reasons, the team members must know and understand each other's play and consequently the effective nucleus of the school team may be formed from the members of one class. This may be because the class itself possesses a group of useful players who by dint of regular practice together have developed real co-operation and an understanding of each other's play. It is well worth while stimulating small groups in senior classes to work in this way so that possible team units may be produced.

Again, from experience I have found it advisable to have a squad of players rather than a mere team unit. Additions can always be made to the numbers in the squad, and on many occasions the boys themselves recommend useful players. Within the total squad, the group principle of having smaller units who play with real understanding still operates, and in the 1960–1 E.S.B.B.A. season, when Hertfordshire won the junior championship, five boys in the team came from one class.

In time it would be most desirable to have a school squad for each year so that a group of top players is always available to move up and form the new team at the end of the year. This, of

61

course, necessitates plenty of games for the up and coming players and presents a staffing problem.

There is obviously quite an amount of skill in choosing and balancing the team from the main squad. Several factors must be borne in mind and these include the ability and size of the players, the tactics to be employed and also the ability and make-up of the opposing teams which will be encountered. The small boys in the group are usually the most agile; they pick up the game quickly and soon become real exponents of the fast break. Height, however, is of great importance and it is foolish to ignore the tall lad. Height at an early age brings with it a disconcerting difficulty in co-ordination and this may mean that the tall boy who has real basketball potential is somewhat of a passenger in the early days of his playing. If he shows potential, however, he should be persevered with, for as soon as he begins to 'fill out' he will become a real asset to the team. Since he towers above his fellows he may be quite lazy as regards jumping and specific exercises should be given to improve his jumping ability. Perhaps the best treatment, if this is possible, is to have another equally tall boy on the squad. This will produce real competition between the two and the honours will go to the better jumper.

The good set shooter has a very special skill. He is usually a cool-headed and careful lad, insistent upon good form yet ready to take his chances as and when they occur. This type of boy must be encouraged more than any other player in the team for he must practise his set shooting over long periods. It takes time to acquire set shooting skill and, once acquired, practice is still necessary to retain it. A team cannot afford to have its set shooter off form since on so many occasions the attack is built around the steady work of the set shooter.

Somewhere in the team must be fitted the final 'interlocking piece'. He is the boy with the superior knowledge of the game and he usually becomes the playmaker. He knows when to play as safety man and when to go through if the fast attack has broken down; he may even be the high post or pivot player. Preferably, however, he should be a guard who moves into a safety or balance position from which he can dictate the control and run of play. Such boys are born leaders and are anxious to gain as much knowledge of the game as possible and then to put the knowledge to good use.

It may seem a tall order to find and train boys to this ability and this standard but if basketball of quality is going to be produced in the school, then work and thought are necessary. The effort is, after all, no more than that extended to the cricket or soccer team and their various dispositions.

SPECIAL TRAINING

When the squad has been collected together, then the scheme of training will be planned according to the tactics which the coach has in mind. The practices and the aim behind the training must be slightly different from the work done in the usual basketball lesson. The squad must be made to feel that their training is with a definite purpose of mind and that one purpose is to blend each individual to fit into a particular style of play. This helps to develop a pride in play and will serve to cut out regular absences from training. It will also get rid of the prima donna type of player who is often far more trouble than he is worth.

The team session is an excellent opportunity to work over all the skills that are difficult to operate with large classes—i.e. screens, picks, blocking out, etc. Once these skills have been mastered it will be found that the various players will put them to good use in class games and the result will be that the brighter members of class teams will try to imitate these new points. This can become a wonderful example of the squad setting a higher standard of basketball throughout the school. Moreover, if the squad itself is chosen from all the eligible classes, the spread of advanced skills will penetrate over a greater part of the school.

As the game develops within the school there comes the question regarding the organization of an Inter-Mural League. This may be based on the house system but from recent experiments it has been my experience to find that the class provides a closer knit unity and makes for a much better supported side. As an experiment, three separate class teams were entered in the district schools under-fourteen league and all acquitted themselves well. The boys themselves seemed anxious to support their own class, but more important still, each boy in the class seemed to think that he was personally close to participation in competitive basketball.

OUTSIDE COMPETITION

First-year boys need a good grounding in the fundamentals before they come to their first real match. It is often sufficient to sustain their interest if an occasional game is arranged against their contemporaries in another school. The later in the season that these matches are organized, the better it is, for the boys have had more time to assimilate the various aspects of the game. They come to their first match with much more polish. In the second year, it is advisable to arrange more matches, still on a friendly basis and preferably according to an agreement which can be easily altered. In spite of careful training, the first game may show up a number of glaring faults which must be righted. If a predetermined succession of games has been arranged there may not be an opportunity to fit in the necessary coaching to eradicate these faults. During the second year, the young players will improve by leaps and bounds. They will consolidate their rhythm of play and advance sufficiently so that by the third year they may be well enough prepared to compete in a local school league.

Probably one of the major facets of succeeding in any game is to build that particular game into the tradition of the school. In a young game like basketball it is often a good idea to start competition with one's local schools but not to be afraid to branch out and search farther afield for good opposition. This may entail a great deal of travelling but it will repay in experience and exchange of ideas. Playing other schools within the county often brings boys into contact with future county team mates whilst out-county games give the boys even wider horizons. In order to 'talk basketball' they must have experience of seeing and even playing against county and national standard players.

Many senior clubs have difficulty in obtaining new player material and here a contact could be made with a view to placing young players when they leave school. The tie which brings senior experience, qualified coaching and outside contact with the national body can be most useful. If there is any problem about post-school play, the school players may wish to continue as a club when they leave school. Future administrative and refereeing problems may be overcome by training boys for these posts whilst they are at school as part of the general tradition.

The basic training and practice for young referees can take place during games periods and house matches, with an occasional classroom lesson on rule interpretation. Youngsters can take A.B.B.A. courses and qualifications at virtually any age and there are many sixteen-year-olds blowing whistles and declaiming the rules in local leagues.

Publicity of the game both within school and outside are additional spurs to the players and must not be ignored. Because of the fact that it is indoors, spectators will flock to watch a school basketball match in far larger numbers than to a soccer match. Basketball provides speed of incident, particularly in a close game and this helps to maintain a high standard of interest. The presence of spectators in school gymnasia certainly makes for added difficulties, nevertheless an audience is well worth while for enthusiasm is created and the many niceties of play are applauded and probably copied on a later occasion.

Basketball in schools seems to develop an interest and enthusiasm which is rarely shown by any of the other sports. It may be because it is a new game and so something of a novelty but there may be other far deeper reasons which include such factors as an urgent desire by all boys to play the game and play it well. The development of basketball can do a great deal to make the gymnasium a real centre for crowded activity in the school; this surely speaks well for the game, and demonstrates one of the major uses of the gymnasium.

4

THE NATIONAL TEAM

by G. WILKINSON

THE CHANGING WORLD

Years ago the gentry took part in sport for the love of it, and also because they had the necessary money and leisure time; the working classes played in their spare time, and there was little professionalism. Since those early days, most countries have established more and more sporting relationships, and the importance of world sport has risen to phenomenal heights.

In amateur sport we have the excellent ideals of playing for the game's sake, of getting relaxation and recreation, and developing the qualities of sportsmanship, leadership, graciousness in defeat, modesty in victory, good character, courage and fair play. These are ideals which we admire and which form an important part of our educational system. However, today with the wide coverage given by newspapers and television to world sport, there has been a gradual rise in the importance of results and the prestige gained in international sport. As a result, nations have ensured that for such tournaments as the Olympic Games, their athletes are fully prepared, in a way that is a far cry from the years gone by.

Basketball in Britain, however, is not as advanced in organization as many other nations. Our officers administer the game in their spare time and our players contribute towards training and tournament expenses, and rely on the goodwill of many people for efficient development. Working under such handicaps, it is more difficult to produce a national team of high calibre capable of competing with the highly subsidized teams of other nations.

THE NATIONAL TEAM

To do the job of coaching properly a national coach should be a full-time professional. He must be a man of many parts, for the art of coaching requires a great deal more than just a knowledge of how the game is played. If anyone is to become such a coach, he should have in his possession a good working knowledge of the following:

(*i*) A basic understanding of the human body and how it functions, for this will enable him to understand the terrific potential of the human machine. This is a very wide subject and covers anatomy, physiology, kinesiology, diet and first-aid. Players must be trained to become 'fit for basketball', so the coach must know what is meant by such terms as strength, endurance, stamina, skill, fatigue—to mention a few.

(*ii*) The modern methods used to give the hard basic core of fitness which every player should have. He should know what preparation is required for the start of a new season and what work is necessary during the season. He must understand such things as weight training, circuit training, strengthening exercises, endurance exercises and the exercises ideal for development of the muscle groups and organs used mainly by the basketball player.

(*iii*) How to plan programmes and sessions, whether they be for beginners or internationals, or for teachers or coaches.

(*iv*) How to teach, coach and lecture. Here, teaching is regarded as the training of persons in something new to them, something they are learning to do for the first time; coaching follows teaching in that, after being taught, the pupil is kept on the right track of performing the skill he is practising. The pupil understands what is to be done, but as he cannot see his own performance, the coach acts as a camera or eye, seeing, analysing and giving the pupil the points to develop or correct. The art of teaching, coaching and lecturing is again a very wide study. It covers among other things, basic psychology. A teacher must possess many of the qualities of an actor, and be able to command and lead; he must have a fine sense of drama and emphasis, and also have the ability to portray humour, seriousness, anger, pleasure and many other emotions to obtain his aim. He must have the personality to impress people and make them listen to him. He must have a good basic ability at his trade and be able to demonstrate at a reasonable level. The coach who can demonstrate and who shows great enthusiasm and fitness will gain considerable respect from his pupils. If a coach does not have sufficient skill or is handicapped by age, then he should use a technically sound player to demonstrate for him.

(v) A comprehensive knowledge of the aims of basketball and the rules and interpretations, for in teaching many of the techniques it is important to understand fully the rules concerning them.

In addition, the coach must really be up to date on the theories and practices of the game. This knowledge is gained largely through the 'picking of brains', either by reading all the available literature, or by listening to, questioning, discussing basketball with other coaches at every available opportunity.

Lastly, a coach must bear in mind the future good of the game. He should try to present to the public an entertainment and spectacle of athletic ability, grace, skill and strategy. He is responsible for his team's conduct and reputation. If a coach has the knowledge and principles mentioned, then with ambition and luck he can achieve success for himself and at the same time do a lot for the future success of basketball.

THE INTERNATIONAL PLAYER

When a player achieves his ambition and is honoured by being selected to represent his country, he immediately assumes a new status, which carries with it certain responsibilities and obligations.

Players and spectators alike will expect a high degree of skill from him and if he falls short of these standards he will cause not only himself but the game as well to fall into some disrepute. The international player is a standard bearer for the game, and an example for all other striving aspirants.

A most important feature of his make up should be his sportsmanship and his attitude towards basketball generally; his relationship with officials, opponents, team mates, and spectators must always be on a good plane. A person's character can frequently be read by the way in which he plays a game, and all too often outstanding players, internationals perhaps, are guilty of fits of temperament and petulant acts towards officials and opponents. Unfortunately, these mannerisms and characteristics are sometimes imitated by other members of the team. Imitation is one of the basic ways of learning, so international players must be particularly careful of their conduct, no matter what standard or how little importance is attached to the game in which they may be playing. In international tournaments, bad sportsmanship is rarely seen but this is probably because the player, when he is with his national team is more aware of his responsibilities. Moreover, the coach has a strong grip on his team and will not tolerate any disreputable act, and the officials are of a high calibre and will readily clamp down on any awkward player. At club level and in minor games there is not so much control and the reputable player, who may be an international, will often seek to gain some advantage over the officials. Fortunately, the majority of our international players, particularly the more experienced ones, have matured, and set a fine example to anyone watching. This is, of course, how it should be, and how everyone expects it to be.

BASKETBALL FITNESS

All potential internationals must strive to achieve the high standard of 'fitness for basketball' required for international tournaments. To reach and maintain this very demanding level, players should be playing constantly in top class games; they should practise twice a week, train regularly with colleagues from the international team, follow a routine physical fitness programme and do the greater part of this under the guidance of the club coach and the national coach. How does competition in this country measure up to this? The London League has the highest standard in England, but by and large the courts are poor and the modified courts of such excellent clubs as the Polytechnic and Central Y.M.C.A. do not demand, and so do not develop, a really high degree of fitness. The League does not compare in standard with say, the leading continental leagues. We are, as coach Jim

McGregor, an American who has coached in many countries, remarked, 'surrounded by the Channel curtain'. This lack of contact with continental countries is unfortunate, because good and consistent continental opposition would do a lot to the raising of our standards.

Playing the game is not enough and our best players must do some extra training to develop strength and endurance; moreover the coach must include weight training and circuit training as part of the general programme. Basketball players in England do very little of this sort of work compared with athletes, soccer players, or swimmers, and more attention should be given to these subjects in the A.B.B.A. examinations for coaches. It is obvious from the way that certain continental teams warm up that they are trained and efficient athletes as well as highly skilful basketball players. The general fitness training done by some continental teams is as powerful and demanding as that used by any top class track or field athlete.

It is obvious that our players must study this question of fitness, and our coaches must make it a very important part of their research if we are to put it in its proper perspective and deal adequately with it. International players must be in a really sound condition for the tremendous demands of such tournaments as the Olympics, and European Games. The standard can only be acquired by a lot of hard, demanding work, a dedicated approach and expert guidance and tuition. Skill in training must go hand in hand with endurance training for skills must still be performed when fatigue is setting in. Fatigue affects skill and towards the end of a hard and strenuous game, even the most skilful players miss easy chances, or make fundamental mistakes; all too often these mistakes occur because of fatigue affecting the skill factor.

When practising skills it is advisable to perform them vigorously and strenuously in the same manner as in a game. Endurance, or the ability to withstand fatigue, will thus be developed, and in this way players will be training to meet actual game situations. The two most strenuous aspects of basketball are, of course, running and jumping, consequently most practices should incorporate these movements. In addition drills must be made highly competitive, and ideally should be between groups of evenly matched players. The following are examples of drills worked out in this manner:

Lay-up shot practice. The players are organized in twos. One player dribbles the ball slowly to the centre court, with his opponent close behind him; on reaching the centre the dribbler makes a sudden dive for basket, and the rear man chases him and tries to block his shot. The

6. Lay-up shot

defender secures the ball and starts a slow dribble back to the centre, with the previous shooter falling in behind him; the practice continues in this way.

Jump shot practice. A 'pressure drill'. The shooter is on the free throw line with a defender between him and the basket. Two feeders each with a ball stand at an angle of 45° to the shooter. Under the basket are two retrievers with a ball each. Alternatively the feeders pass to the shooter who must move, receive the pass and shoot over the guard. The retrievers pass to the feeders. The shooter must rebound every shot and if he secures the rebound he must try to score. He then turns to receive the next pass. The drill is continuous, with the defender playing all out.

'*A one on one game.*' The group works in pairs and each pair plays a full court game. This gives practice in all fundamentals with the exception of passing.

'*One on one driving drill.*' An attacker has the ball at centre court, with a defender at the top of the free throw arc. When the attacker starts to drive the defender can play him in any fashion.

'*One on one drill.*' An attacker is at the top of the free throw arc, with a defender under the ring with the ball. The defender passes the ball and chases after it. The attacker practises immediate shots, or up and under plays.

An important feature in all these drills is the rebounding of the shots. The drills also give practice in offence and defence and if the players really compete against each other, a great deal of hard physical work is done; many repetitions of these types of practices will develop endurance whilst the skill factor is present, just as it is in an actual game.

An international must build up his general endurance by using drills and practices that entail a considerable amount of running. In the Royal Air Force team, several of the fittest players take part in such events as cross country and as a result have very few worries regarding lasting even the toughest games, or having their skill effected by fatigue. The R.A.F. players include jumping exercises in their circuit training and general training; these exercises are very strenuous but most essential.

International players should, when at their peak of fitness, neither take alcohol nor smoke, and hard though it may seem, smoking and 'drinking' should be stopped.

SELECTING THE NATIONAL TEAM

The business of selecting a national team is a most responsible and by no means an easy task. There is a diversity of opinion regarding the best method and each country tends to approach the problem in a different way. Factors such as the size of the country, the standard of basketball and the financial position of the national association, all have bearing on the system used.

THE NATIONAL TEAM

SELECTORS

There are likewise many opinions regarding the ideal number of people who should constitute the selection committee. In certain countries, not only in basketball, but in other team games as well, considerable success has been achieved by giving the task of selecting the national team to one man. This could be a very good system provided that this man possesses the qualifications and qualities for the job. Such a man must be a person of high integrity and character, he must have a tremendous amount of experience, information and knowledge of all facets of his nation's basketball, and what is so important, he must be a full-time professional, who has as part of his responsibility the development of the national team. In the absence of such a person it is advisable to have a selection committee. This should not be a big, unwieldy committee and should consist of not more than five men; between them they should have contact with basketball throughout the country. The national coach should be a member of the committee and as he has the task of training and coaching the team, he should give to the committee a synopsis of his aims and requirements for the games ahead, with such information that he may have regarding the opposition and the conditions to be met.

When nominating selectors, certain references and qualities should be considered. A selector must have had active experience in the game either as a player or as a coach, for it is useless choosing someone who has merely been a spectator.

Selectors will always be criticized and accused of favouritism and bias. This they must accept philosophically, provided that they know that they have been fair-minded and wise in their choice. Their aim, which must all the time be kept in view, is to select the best possible team to represent the country.

TRIALS

In the home countries a system of holding trials is used and this is without doubt the only system applicable. In America, a winning team will form the majority of a national team, the remaining

73

places being filled by exceptional players from other teams. It is difficult for the Americans to use our system because of their high standard of play and the large numbers of players of a similar standard competing for just a few places. In Britain however, it is necessary for preliminary trials to be held in suitable places, so that players can be chosen who will go forward for the final trial. In addition, representative games must be arranged to give these players an opportunity working together as a team. On occasions like this the opposition should be a particularly strong unit for only in games of this calibre can unknown players be compared with young potential aspirants to international honours.

During the selection, the complete make up of the team must be considered so that a balanced team is finally selected. A team going to such tournaments as the Olympics must have at least four pivots, four forwards and four guards. Within these groups, the players again will differ in that some will have a flair for offence and others for defence, but all players, however, should have the correct attitude towards defence. A team must also have star players who can score under any conditions; these players are usually forwards who can shoot from the outside and also be effective close to basket.

Certain definite factors should be uppermost in the minds of the selectors when they are considering their choice, and the team should be picked with these points in mind. Basketball is a game where the advantage is with the tall man and if one of these is a star scorer then he will be invaluable to the team and to the coach. Every coach would like such a player in his team, but there is a shortage in British basketball, of big men who can run and jump in a similar fashion to our smaller men.

In every team there must be a 'general'. He should be captain of the team, and is best positioned as a 'quarter back'. He is a person who is a born leader, who 'reads' a game well, who understands his coach thoroughly, and delights in controlling the speed of the game, particularly during tense moments and crises. He is looked upon as the brains of the team, and usually has more of the ball than anyone, possibly gaining greater satisfaction in creating a basket than in scoring one. Another necessary player is the man who might be called the 'inspiration'. He may play in any position, but usually he is a guard, and takes a pride in his defence. He is always first back to stop the break; he doesn't know what it is to give in. His interceptions, his diving for loose balls, his 'hawking' and the look he gives his coach when substituted, all make him into an inspiration. His enthusiasm and his fight, have a 'carry over' value to the whole team, and can stimulate them to greater things.

There is a real need for a star scorer. He is usually a forward who possesses a fine physique, and takes a great pride in his fitness. He has command of many shots and can score from the inside as well as the outside. He competes with the big men as a rebounder by virtue of his athletic ability, for he is able to leap like a gazelle. He can drive through a wall; has a jump shot from over twenty feet and is too good a passer to double team. Every team has to consider a special plan to stop him, and his name precedes him wherever he goes.

Not often noted, but invaluable to a team are the 'unselfish ones' or utility men; they are the men who can be relied upon for the same performance each time; they get great satisfaction in acting as obstruction men, screening for the star scorer and marking star opponents. These men are often the most liked men in the team, and so they should be.

Conducting Trials

It is essential that trials are planned with a considerable amount of forethought. If a player in a trial is opposed by an experienced man, he may give a poor showing, and vice versa, consequently there should be numerous switchings and changing of players so that everyone has a fair trial. If time is short, a good method is to see the established men who are near certainties, for a brief period only. When they have given confirmation of their ability they should be taken out of the game so that the rest of the players can be switched around. Usually at a final trial there will be some twenty players. If six of these are international stars, whom everyone agrees should be chosen, it leaves fourteen players for the remaining six places. These fourteen are then played in a variety of chosen patterns and the standards compared with each other. Where doubt exists, these players can be given a turn against one of the chosen six, and on this performance a final impression gained. After a good amount of play, any person not obviously up to standard can be taken out of the game.

During trials, man-to-man defence should be played, for this is the one most usually encountered in international games. Moreover, man-to-man defence shows individual defensive and offensive ability. In some methods of defence a defender can 'hide', and in offence against a zone, a player can handle the ball so much more easily because he is under less pressure.

One important feature when finalizing selection is that it is not necessary to name the full team if the committee have doubt over players for the last remaining places. For the European games, the English committee nominated eight players, and then gave the remaining players a game in a representative match before naming the last four places. This method of utilizing representative games is an excellent manner of seeing players under actual game conditions. Trials are a little artificial and not everyone feels at home in them, as they possibly would in a game. Such qualities as match temperament are not always seen to the best advantage in a trial.

BRITISH TEAMS AND CONTINENTAL TEAMS

It has been possible during recent years for English or British representative teams to take part in international competitions. Tournaments of this type give a much more accurate picture of the relative standard of our game than do the occasional international matches against other countries. It is possible as a result of such festivals to learn a great deal about the game development in other countries and to assess the position of basketball in the general popularity ranking of the various sports.

During competitions like the European tournaments when a large number of representative teams are together for several days, the many teams can be watched during training periods, and discussions are possible between the coaches themselves on the efficacy of coaching methods. A great deal has been learned in this way about continental play and continental training and even though the English team has sometimes been lowly placed in the competitions, the knowledge gained has been well worth while. At the present moment our attitude must be to pick up basketball knowledge from any superior organization or team, and having examined it and sifted it, we must put it to good use if it is to our advantage.

The major factor affecting the differences between our team and the other continental teams lies in the greater importance of basketball in these countries and in the high prestige value gained by good results at international tournaments. The popularity of basketball in certain countries can be judged from the fact that in Yugoslavia the Sportsman of the Year in 1961 was their basketball Pivot! At present it seems unbelievable that one of our players will ever attain this honour! In addition, our politicians and leading statesmen still upohold the best traditions of amateurism and all the ideals behind it, and our Government will not apparently subsidize sport in the same way that other countries do. The result is that our teams are not so well equipped nor have as much training time available to them as continental teams. The overall picture is not only financial but concerns playing space as well. Our playing facilities are improving, but they could be better utilized, and greater co-operation should exist between Local Authorities, Local Education Authorities and the Services so that the best accommodation could be available and used to the full. Another development would be to organize outdoor basketball in the summer, and it would be a simple matter to find suitable spacious areas in which to play the game. In Belgium, basketball has developed by leaps and bounds since the teams decided to play outdoors; they even operate in winter with a climate similar to ours! In the 1960 pre-Olympic tournament, Belgium was narrowly defeated by Spain and Hungary and just missed qualification for the Olympics. Belgian basketball has been practised and played for the most part, out of doors. One thing is sure! We shall have to make many experiments and changes if we are to progress. Our facilities in general are stunting the growth and development of the game in this country.

Another important difference between the continental teams and English teams is usually the superior athletic ability and fitness of the foreign players. At the moment our average international player does not meet up to the standard of such teams as Hungary or Poland. There are many reasons for this, but one reason is probably that we are not getting the best athletes to play the game. We must sell basketball to our track athletes, our soccer players and our rugby players; all too often the people taking part in basketball are those who cannot make the soccer or rugby team. One cannot expect good athletes to make an immediate change-over to a new and foreign sport, and one of the best methods of getting them interested and playing basketball is to advise them to use it as a means of training for their first love. In Russia and America, for example, many stars of their other national games play basketball. Methods like this will certainly make basketball popular with athletes of good ability.

Our top players do not give enough serious consideration to fitness and it must again be emphasized that if a person is to play for his country he is obligated to reach the best condition he can with the knowledge and facilities he has at hand. Physical educationalists and coaches can help by publicizing the methods of fitness training which are of particular value to the modern basketball player. This should certainly make all players to be more fitness conscious.

The majority of the continental players have a much higher standard of skill than our players, but their team strategies and patterns of play are not intricate or elaborate; it is apparent that in this direction new methods are not being used. The main defence employed is man-to-man and the main offensive pattern seems to be the 2–2–1 formation. The outstanding impression gained whilst watching international competitions is the superb performances of the basic fundamental skills. Many words could be written on this particular aspect alone but I will just dwell on some continental techniques which provide new ideas on coaching.

When a pass was made to the pivot player, the latter used a high overhead ball handling position. This position is not difficult to learn, and it can soon prove to be of considerable value not only to the pivot but to many other players. A lot of the better rear court ball handlers can employ a two-handed set shot from this high position, for as the ball is carried high, it becomes a difficult shot to block. In reaching to block, the defender is often caught out with a fake shot and drive, or as it is more commonly called the 'up and under'.

The pivots, in shooting, used what may be called an 'up and in' technique. They did not fade away with their shot but leapt up and in towards the basket, jumping with great power. When shooting with the outside hand, a hook or turn around jump shot would be used, but the favourite was to use the inside hand with the 'up and in' technique. The aim with this technique was first, two points, secondly to draw a foul, and thirdly, to secure the rebound. In contrast, if the pivot fades away as he shoots he may score but he is moving away from the ball and so has less chance of being fouled and no opportunity to take the rebound.

Individual defence had obviously formed a large part of the training schedules. Since the defender has such a great disadvantage with the present interpretation of the rules, a pivot defender cannot be expected to guard the pivot without help. Each player, therefore, was conscious of giving help whenever he could to his team mate and in particular his pivot defender. Sagging tactics were employed by most teams. The main defence used was man-to-man defence.

AIMS AND IDEALS FOR THE FUTURE

Progress is not something that happens overnight. There may be decisions and landmarks that make for sudden change, but in the main the progress of a new sport is a rather slow operation. To date, scant headway has been made and the keen and fanatical followers of basketball in this country feel frustrated and futile; to them, the game seems to be virtually at a standstill.

It is true that there are now many more teams operating in local leagues and the organization within these leagues is improving. The standard of play is still not good, and the 'man in the street' who may call in to see these games must take away a poor opinion of basketball.

Members of local leagues and local clubs are particularly busy people and quite often they bear the full responsibility of league administration and organization, as well as taking part in and officiating the game. They have little time available for the 'staging' of matches and this very important aspect is neglected. Consequently, basketball is not always 'presented' to the public as a spectacle or as an interesting game, and so it remains hidden and obscure, watched perhaps by a mere handful of friends and relations of the players themselves. Even for these few spectators, there is often little comfort and they usually have to sit on improvised seating in such close proximity to the players that at times their presence may be quite a liability.

To remedy this state of affairs, every club should consider appointing a publicity officer whose sole job is to 'sell' the game to the public. If he does his duty properly, an officer of this type will soon have a busy time, for he must ensure that games start promptly, that teams are well turned out and that the seating accommodation provided for spectators is as comfortable as possible. The stage is then set at the court for the reception of spectators; his next duty is to encourage these people to come along. To do this, he enlists the help of the players to bring parents, friends, or girl friends to see the various matches. He will also make certain that special games are arranged which should attract a bumper crowd and that on such occasions the game is properly explained to the audience. Reports and results of games, together with current league tables should appear regularly in the local press and in these various ways a following for the game will be built up.

We must not be complacent about the general publicity aspect; other countries have made basketball a sport which commands a big spectator following. It is even claimed by American statiticians that the game has more players and more spectators than any other sport in the world. In Russia, China, Europe and the Americas, basketball is one of the top games and has a vast number of supporters.

There have been some developments in England towards better basketball even though it may appear that the impact on clubs has been small. The greatest achievement during recent years has been the forming of schoolboy, youth and junior teams, at national level, and the start of their associations. Here surely lies the future of basketball, for when a sport is firmly entrenched as an integral part of school life, then given time, it must succeed and gain in popularity. It is wonderful to see outdoor basketball stands in playgrounds around the country; to basketball enthusiasts, they show themselves as a landmark of progress. The game is becoming very popular in the services and there have been plenty of signs and results to show the march of progress. It is interesting to note that the Royal Air Force team which used to be thrashed by all American services teams in this country can now hold its own with the majority of these teams. We no longer look upon the Americans as unbeatable as was the case some years ago, and the American players themselves are remarking on the tremendous improvement they have seen occur in just one season.

There are certain vital factors, however, which are essential for the improvement of basketball in this country. These can be briefly summarized as follows:

1. We must try to improve the financial position of our national association, for without money it is difficult to prepare and send teams in a proper fashion to major tournaments. A special committee with the sole aim of raising money should be set up to deal with this situation. The members of this committee should take it upon themselves to see that the player's expenses are paid for him. This finance committee could cover the whole of the country from a geographical point of view and the members should discuss at committee meetings, every possible method of raising funds.

2. We must make a determined attempt to break the 'Channel Curtain'. There are obvious difficulties in this and one of the main ones is directly concerned with finance. If, however, we are going to gain experience and improve our standard of play we must play the continental teams. Competition is the best way to learn and improve, and we must assess the results of such competition as our measure of progress. We all know that to improve we must play teams which are slightly superior and we must play them regularly.

3. We must seek competition with as many American service teams in this country as we can, and preferably play on their courts! The Americans are without doubt the strongest community of basketball, and we are not taking full advantage of this. Something has been done about this during the last few years but many more and better relationships could be made.

4. We must all try to organize regular tournaments of a good

standard and if the public won't come to us, then the games must be played where people cannot fail to see them. The summer provides the best opportunities for such games, and tournaments can be organized in parks and open spaces and at seaside resorts. Where accommodation is suitable, there can be big gatherings of teams for indoor tournaments, in fact at Cosford, near Wolverhampton, over a hundred ten-minute games in such a competition have been played in a day! These projects will do a world of good to basketball, and may even become the life blood of the game. American teams can provide the public appeal in tournaments of this kind.

5. The blooding of our youngsters to the international scene by the organization of junior internationals and 'Under 20' games, is a policy that must ensure success for future senior teams. This system provides an ideal progression and helps youngsters to mature properly. It is entirely wrong for a new senior international player to be rushed into the hotbed of such tournaments as the Olympics with no previous experience of this standard of play. The progression from the schoolboy to the Under 18s, then to the Under 20s, and finally to the senior team will prevent this from occurring.

6. Our long-term policy must be to establish several full-time professional coaches. They would be responsible for national clinics for both coaches and players, and would devise a policy which would be adhered to by the assistant coaches responsible for the youth and schoolboy teams. In this way the young players would become acquainted with the methods employed by the senior team at a very early stage in their career, and they would obtain consistent training in established principles and methods.

7. Our general attitude should be to work for the best possible relationships with industries, schools and the services so that full use is made of their facilities and potential. In all three cases, there are vast untapped sources of basketball ability awaiting the inspiration to play, and prepared to follow a well-conducted coaching scheme. Players are not there just for the asking but sufficient and well-organized work presented in an attractive way will win players and supporters who will do honour to the game.

Finally, I would like to say that basketball in Britain has now obtained a very firm footing and will soon be known by all and sundry here at home. It is a fine game that has succeeded throughout the world and as time will show, will succeed here. Generations change in their tastes, some of our national sports are declining, and the younger and more modern sports are coming to the fore. Basketball is one of the latter, and I hope that all associated with the game will do their utmost to promote the sport, and bring it to the top.

5

BASKETBALL OFFICIATING

by W. A. TAYLOR

Basketball is a game played between two teams of five players, and the whole object of the game is to 'throw' the ball from any- where on the court in such a way that it passes through the basket. This sounds very easy, of course, but the phrase 'subject to certain conditions' which occurs in the opening paragraph of the rule book, imposes definite regulations to which every player must submit. To administer these regulations efficiently it is necessary to have another team which consists of a captain, a vice-captain, two 'secretaries' and one other helper. Their correct titles are the Referee, Umpire, Scorer, Timekeeper and Thirty-second Operator. This team will never score a basket but nevertheless all members are important and necessary for the proper conduct of a game.

These various people have many duties, and here the word people has been used purposely in deference to the number of ladies who act so efficiently as scorers and timekeepers for clubs around the country. Amongst the group, the referee and umpire are the most important and they occupy the main roles of chief officials. For their duties they need training and experience but there are certain other unwritten laws with which they must comply. They must be physically fit, for basketball is a fast game, and it is essential to keep up with the play. Nothing annoys a good player more than to have an official 'blowing' for things which he cannot possibly see because he has been too lazy to maintain his correct position. Officials have a strenuous period during a basketball game and when the game is over they should leave the court with a certain amount of physical fatigue and a considerable amount of mental fatigue.

It is vital that the officials are 100 per cent impartial in their decisions. The man who has a 'down' on certain players will never be successful, and moreover his attitude may so influence some players that they are completely knocked off their game during the period of the match. Officials should therefore approach all games in a natural and efficient manner and they must always have the courage of their convictions to call fairly for things which contravene the rules. Quite often during games, officials show by their reactions that they have seen fouls or violations, yet no call is made. The situation is much worse when such an occurrence takes place just before a basket is scored. Immediately there is an atmosphere of dissension prevalent amongst the players, and it is from situations like these that such remarks as, 'How about that Ref?' or, 'What about the foul, Ref?' are shouted across the court. It is entirely wrong for a player to have to indicate to the official that an obvious foul has occurred, for this definitely implies a loss of faith in the officiating. Nevertheless, whatever the feelings of the referee may be, if he has seen the foul or violation he must swallow his pride and call the proper penalty even though it would appear that he has been reminded of his duties by a player.

Correct attire is important for officials, and they should take some pride in dressing properly for their duties. Naturally, each game doesn't warrant the full treatment of 'grey this and grey that', but nevertheless, a neat and tidy uniform is important for all games. Obviously at games of premier status, officials should be dressed according to the book.

KNOWLEDGE OF THE RULES

The above points covering fitness, impartiality and dress help to make and maintain an efficient and respected official, but so far the main requirements have not been mentioned. These are a complete knowledge of the rules and a thorough competence in their administration. Omissions in knowledge can lead to most awkward situations and it often applies that these weak spots are shown up at critical points in important matches. Imagine, for instance, the scene at the local Derby to decide who progresses into the national section of the A.B.B.A. Championships; Whites, who are one point down score a basket but whilst the ball is in flight, a Red player is deliberately fouled, and the timekeeper gives the signal for the end of the game! All referees from the lowest grade upwards will at some time have to deal with a situation of this sort and they can only handle it properly if they are complete masters of the rules and have an official and quiet way of administering these rules.

PREPARATION FOR MATCHES

As a general rule in this country, officials tend to consider that special preparation for basketball games is not necessary. This does not imply that they do not make any preparation but by and large the preparatory work tends to be skimped. In many cases there are extenuating circumstances, for the majority of officials have to do a day's work in the factory, the mine or the office. Immediately this is over, there is the rush home, a change of clothes, a quick meal and then probably the journey straight out to the game. Many officials who have to organize things in this way are truly devoted to the game and have little opportunity for anything more than scant preparation. Nevertheless, some attention must be given to equipment and it is very true that as officials improve and administer better games, the more careful must be this advance preparation.

Fortunately, apart from personal gear, there is not a lot of equipment needed. The main thing, of course, is the whistle and it is advisable to obtain two whistles, both of which have a fairly high-pitched tone. This means, that the whistles will have to be tested before they are purchased and although this may seem strange, the shopkeeper usually offers no objection. Whistles with higher pitched tones are chosen because they ensure a quicker player reaction. These two whistles should become the absolute personal property of the official and he should allow no one else to borrow them or to use them. Although it may appear somewhat extravagant, it is advisable to have a third whistle which can be the 'borrowing' one; this can be available if the appointed co-official fails to turn up and the services of another person have to be employed.

It is sound advice to be sensible about the type and quantity of food eaten before a game. Obviously the official has to feel comfortable during the period of the game and a light meal taken an hour to an hour and a half prior to the centre jump should be adequate.

Kit should be laundered regularly, for, as we have seen, the neat and tidy appearance of the referee is important. Special attention should be given to the socks and boots. Badly fitting socks or socks that are not clean will cause foot blisters and these will greatly hamper the official in the proper performance of his duties. Boots are often neglected, and after a game are put away damp with perspiration or even worse, wet from proximity to the shower. The time spent seeing that the boots are clean and dry is well worth while.

THE GAME DUTIES

It is part of the referee's responsibility to see that everything is in order at the court itself so that he can start the game on time, and with every assurance that the equipment is adequate for the occasion. This means that the officials should be at the court at least half an hour before the game is scheduled to start. There are several pre-game duties, and these include an inspection of all the court equipment and the immediate surroundings. The officials must check to see that the backboards are supported adequately, that the baskets are properly secured and the nets are firmly tied down all the way round. Too many teams are content with nets that are hung in a slovenly way and the officials are doing a good service to both teams by insisting that the nets be put into their proper position and fixed. A quick inspection must be made of the court boundaries. The majority of courts in this country are of the non-regulation type and the various projections such as overhanging beams, roof supports or anything else which is liable to interfere with the flight of the ball, must be noted. The two officials must get together and decide what is to be done when the ball hits a projection, and their various decisions have to be made known to the captains and coaches of the teams. While captains and coaches are present it is a good idea to remind them that players must raise their hands and face the 'table' when a foul is called against them, and that they must also stay off court during substitution until they are given permission to enter. This may be the nearer official but if this person is tied up with the administration of a jump ball, or a free throw then the other official can undertake these duties. The coaches can also be reminded that they have the responsibility of furnishing the scorer with the names and details of the teams; the coach of the home side can be told to leave the two match balls near to the 'table' and questions can be raised to see that colours do not clash. If all this is done some little time before the scheduled start of the game, there is still time to make minor alterations and yet make a punctual start.

Captains and coaches can now be dismissed and this will give an opportunity for the two officials to be together to check that they both follow the system of officiating approved by the A.B.B.A. In so many instances where the officials are old friends or both wear A.B.B.A. badges, this may not be necessary, but where the co-official is a stranger then a quick word on this point may save embarrassment during the game.

The officials must also have a short conference with the scorer, timekeeper and thirty-second operator. These three men must maintain their duties throughout the game, and their equipment must be approved by the referee. This means in the case of the scorer, the scorebook and his signal; for the timekeeper, the game watch, the numbered cards for fouls, and his signal; and for the thirty-second operator, his equipment and signal. In the presence of all the officials, the referee must check that all signals are understood, for these constitute the main contact with the table whilst the game is in progress.

There should still be a few minutes left before the actual start and during this period the referee will choose the match ball. The bounce test must be done whether a new ball or an old ball is to be used, for the test itself is a rough guide of adequate air pressure. When dropped from a height of six feet, the ball must bounce to a height of four feet, that is mid-chest height of a man five feet ten inches tall. If the ball is in good condition but doesn't do this, then more air must be pumped into it.

All preparations must be complete when the timekeeper gives the three-minute warning. This is an advance notice to both teams and is often used by coaches to select the first five and give them final instructions. When time has one minute to go the referee proceeds to the table, and draws a line under the name of the last player in each team; this is to prevent additions to the team being made after the game has started. The first 'fives' are summoned to positions, a quick check is made to see that five of either side are on court, the floor captains are noted and the game is ready to begin.

It would appear that the pre-game duties are long and arduous, but this is not so. It is advisable, however, that every official establishes a routine for checking all the necessary points and then proceeds thoroughly and methodically through these details. All the points are necessary for all play a part in ensuring that the game will start and continue as a well-organized activity.

DIVISION OF DUTIES

During the actual game each official has specific duties to perform and in the performance of them he assumes particular titles.

1. Active Official. Controls the ball at free throws, jump balls and throws from out of bounds.

2. Free Official. Controls the rest of the court not covered by the active official.

3. Leading Official. During general floor play moves ahead of play.

4. Trailing Official. During general floor play follows play.

At all jump ball situations, the active official always faces the scorer's table and throws the ball up. The free official positions himself on the side line opposite to the active official. He must then lead play whichever direction it goes whilst the active official remains in the circle until play has moved away; he then trails the play.

It is recommended that as a general rule, officials lead to the right and trail to the left. This is customary for people who have been refereeing for some time but newer people may not have the need to revert to this practice. Each official is responsible for the side line nearer to him and approximately two thirds of the end line as leading official. In this way and only in this way can the various violations and fouls which occur during the course of a basketball game be checked and administered. When examined, this method of using a man in front of the ball and a man behind the ball is simple but most effective. The man behind the ball, or trailing man as he is usually known, has for the greater part of the game a clear view of the ball handler. This is because the man with the ball tends to work at the back of the play, and the rest of his colleagues and his opponents are in front of him and nearer to the basket. The trailing official can therefore see the ball handler and the players in his immediate vicinity. The chances are that the nearest player to the ball handler is his particular opponent and these two then become the main focal point of the trailing official's attention; it is around the ball that the violations of travelling and double dribbling and the penalties of personal fouls are likely to occur. There will be incidents away from the ball but since it is in the ball area that things are most likely to go wrong, then this particular area demands the complete attention of one official.

To maintain the 'sandwich' effect, the other official, known as the leading official, will establish himself in front of the ball. The leading official has, however, to maintain vision over a wider area of the court and for the most part he does this by going to a vantage point on the end line of the court. The usual place is adjacent to the spot where the nearer free throw line cuts the end line. From this 'observation point' he can watch the ball handler and his opponent, and all the other players who are in the area in between. He is thus in a good position to see what may happen on a break through to the basket and assess what is taking place in the dangerous area immediately under the basket. Broadly speaking, he watches all the players, even though he concentrates to a fairly large extent on the ball area.

A full and complete observation of the whole court can be obtained in this manner and through this division of duties. The officials have definite focal points to observe during the game and these, as we have seen, are around the ball itself and from the ball area to basket. They should, at the same time, be able to develop their sense of peripheral vision so that they are aware of incidents which may occur away from the ball. Such incidents may be the purposeful fouling of one player by another, or the unlawful contact which follows jockeying for position when an attack is developing. It must be emphasized, however, that there is rarely an absolutely strict division of duties, but the co-operation between the officials should be regarded as an overlapping of duties. This will ensure that there is double supervision of all major and minor incidents in the game.

Further Division of Duties

The division of duties has many further extensions. Each official is mainly responsible for administering out of bounds balls when they occur on his own side line or his end line. There may be occasions, however, when the ball goes out of play near an intersection of responsibility and at such times the officials should co-operate if either has any doubt at all regarding the decision.

On all occasions when a jump ball is called, or a free throw is to be taken, the two officials change sides, and automatically continue duties pertinent to their new position on court. This change must be made efficiently and with full appreciation of the duties of the new position.

The jump ball at the beginning of the game, at the commencement of play in the second half and any subsequent extra periods is done by the referee. Other centre jump balls are performed by the active official, remembering of course that positional exchange will have been made; jump balls at the free throw areas are made by the active official. At the jump ball itself, the official concerned with the tossing up of the ball is responsible for seeing that the restricted area is free from non-jumpers and that players have alternate places on the circle line should they so wish. He then concentrates on the straight toss of the ball to the required height. His vision is therefore upward and limited in range, so he can only watch for personal fouling between the two jumpers from the waist position upwards. His colleague is responsible for fouls following purposeful personal contact by the two jumpers from the waist downwards, for area violation by the non-jumpers and for deliberate personal contact by the non-jumpers.

BASKETBALL OFFICIATING

During a shot for basket, the trailing official watches the flight of the ball and the leading official concentrates on the movement of the players in the area underneath the basket. The division of duties on these occasions is all important, for these are the vital times during a game. The leading official should never see whether the shot has scored, and the full responsibility of witnessing the score and signalling to the scorer's table is entirely with the trailing official.

The active official is responsible for handing the ball over to the player taking a free throw, for watching the flight of the ball to basket and for violations by the free thrower himself. The free official concentrates on violations which may be made by the non-throwers.

There is also a division of duties regarding the time factor rules. The trailing official is responsible for the observation of the thirty second rule and for the five second time allowed to the free thrower. The leading official from his more favourable position watches as a general rule for violations of the three second rule. Each official is responsible for maintaining the five second rule allowed to a team for putting the ball into play from out of bounds.

Game Situations

At the start of the game, the referee takes up his position on the opposite side of the court to the scorer's table. He faces the table and makes a final check with the table officials, then steps into the circle and throws the ball up. As active official he concentrates on the ball and the jumpers. The deliberate action of stepping into the circle indicates to the scorer that the ball is alive. The procedure has already been described in an earlier paragraph headed 'division of duties' and this procedure applies to all jump balls.

The free official becomes the leading official immediately the direction of attack is established and goes quickly to his observation point on the end line concentrating his attention on the ball area and the area between the ball and basket. He is ready for breaks to basket, and rebound plays if a shot is attempted. There are several things likely to happen but the main situations can be listed as follows :

BASKETBALL OFFICIATING

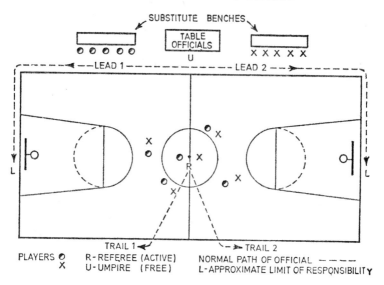

7. Position of officials at start of game

1. A dribbler coming through with the ball and trying for a lay-up shot.

2. A cutter breaking through, receiving the ball and attempting a shot.

3. A long shot followed by defenders and attackers moving in for the rebound.

There will always be a slight variation of pattern but from each of the above accepted ways of attack, certain defensive methods will stand out. The official should, therefore, be especially aware of the developments from the above situations. On all the occasions when one man is trying to beat another, whether the attacker is the ball holder or not, he has only to go round the body of his opponent. The opponent obviously will be guarding with outstretched arms but the particular arm must be dropped as the attacker tries to speed by. The usual method is for the attacker to pass close to the defender aiming to get his head and shoulders ahead of the defender before the defender can turn. If the attacker can do this, subsequent contact is usually the responsibility of the

93

defender. The following movements occur again and again and the official should be especially observant of them:

1. (a) Did the guard move into the path of the dribbling attacker from a close position? If he did so, he has committed the foul.

   (b) Was the guard almost shoulder to shoulder with the dribbling attacker? If there is contact by the guard in this situation, again the guard has fouled.

   (c) Does the guard make contact with the dribbling attacker from behind? This is most definitely a foul.

   (d) If the dribbling attacker runs into the guard who is stationary, then the attacker has fouled.

   (e) If the attacker shoots and then continues his movement forward into a stationary defender, then the attacker has fouled.

2. The cutter is faced with all the same situations as the attacking dribbler, with the addition that deliberate contact made by himself before he receives the ball is a foul committed by him; if he is fouled then the penalty is on the defender.

3. Following any shot at basket, whether it be long, medium or short, there is bound to be considerable contact amongst the players who are in close proximity to the basket area. The players who are 'underneath' the basket and jump fairly straight up for the ball are not likely to foul unless they make awkward bodily movement. It is usually the players outside this area who jump at an angle and consequently go into or come down on opponents, who commit fouls in these situations. In the 'gathering position' before the jump for the rebound, players may deliberately 'hip' an opponent or push him off balance and the leading official must concentrate on these situations and administer the game accordingly.

In all these aspects, unless a player is actually making a shot, contact on the ball holder's hands is allowed, for the hand covering the ball is regarded as part of the ball.

As soon as the official observes deliberate contact or contact which may not be deliberate but nevertheless robs a player of a position of advantage he must automatically blow his whistle. Incident follows incident very quickly in basketball and the official has not time to analyse a situation before he blows the whistle to stop the game. He sees that something has gone wrong, immediately blows the whistle and then analyses. Acting in this way he blows the whistle, assesses the situation and in the briefest fashion explains it. The explanation is always necessary and usually consists of a series of visual signals. We have been considering contact in the basket area so the signals will be in this order:

1. Whistle to stop game.

2. Raise right hand, fist clenched above head. The fist is raised to this position so that it can easily be seen by the timekeeper who stops the clock, the scorer who prepares to make entries in the scorebook, the players and spectators who then know that a foul has been committed:

3. Indicate with index finger of the outstretched arm the player who has committed the foul and see that he faces the score table and raises his hand. This action is so that there can be no doubt as to who committed the foul; it is completed by the official showing, by using his fingers, the number of the player.

4. Indicate to the player who has committed the foul what he was doing. This is done by miming the offence and the action of the mime usually falls into the following categories.

    (*a*) Holding. The signal for any type of holding is one hand clasping the wrist.

    (*b*) Pushing. Whether this is shoulder charging, 'hipping' or pushing with the hands, the signal is shown by holding the hands in front of the body, palms facing outwards and making a definite forward pushing movement with the hands.

    (*c*) Hitting, striking or knocking with hand or arm. The signal is a cutting action with one hand striking against the wrist of the other.

The task of the officials may be easier or harder according to the method of defence used by the defending team. Zone defence makes for a more static game and tends to ease the work of the referee and umpire. Against a man-to-man defence, the officials must be especially aware of screen plays, and they must judge their legality carefully. An attacker may use a front screen where he positions himself in front of a defender to allow a team mate to make a set shot or jump shot over the top. In this situation the officials should watch for any attempt by the 'screen' to hold on to the defender, or by the screen himself extending his arms sideways to prevent the defender getting round to play the ball. If the 'screen' does not stand still in a normal position and at a reasonable distance away from the defender, then he is usually responsible for any personal contact. If, on the other hand, the player who has been screened pushes the 'screen' out of the way in an attempt to reach the ball, then he is the guilty party. He is also guilty if he makes contact by attempting to play over the top of the 'screen'. An attacker may set up a rear screen and in this case he stations himself to the rear or side of a guard. This type of screen movement forms part of the majority of set plays against a man-to-man defence. In the greater number of these instances, physical contact occurs, for the whole idea is to cause the defender to collide with the player who has set the screen. The officials must therefore concentrate on the initial position which is the distance between the screen and the defender. If there is not sufficient room for the defender to move, then the 'screen' is responsible for any contact, but if the 'screen' has left sufficient space, then the defender must make a reasonable attempt to avoid the screen when he follows his man. Negligible contact should be ignored but if the defender deliberately charges the screen out of the way, then he must be penalized.

When playing against man-to-man defence, the attackers usually try to keep the centre lanes open and as a result are not so guilty of violating the three-second rule. They often, however, play a man in the centre pivot position at the place near the top of the restricted area. This player sometimes operates with one foot in and one foot out of the area and if this applies he should be pulled up for violating the three-second rule. A player working in this position with his back to the basket is keenly interested in the whereabouts of his guard and frequently searches the area immediately behind him with one hand to ascertain where the guard is standing. If this movement upsets the guard, but no retaliation is made, the official should warn the attacker and penalize him if he persists.

BALL OUT OF BOUNDS

Out of bounds balls probably create more work for the officials than anything else. As a result it sometimes happens that a degree of complacency creeps into officiating regarding this aspect of their task. This, of course, should never occur and efficiency in all matters must be the aim of both referee and umpire. To administer out of bounds violations, both officials must always be manœuvring so that they are in a good position to be absolutely positive regarding their decisions.

Basically, the decision is very easy to make for if one side cause the ball to go out of play, then the other team return it to play. The important part, however, is to be sure of the responsible team and this demands, as we have emphasized, good position play on behalf of the official, and quick thinking.

As soon as the ball goes out of play, the official must signal the fact with his whistle. He should then move to the place where the violation occurred and indicate with one hand the position from which the ball should be put back into play, and with the other the direction of attack of the team making the throw. All out of bounds balls are now put back into play from the side lines so throw-ins from end-line violations will be from the side line near to the corner.

Where a court is of regulation size and has a six-foot clear area between the boundary lines and the nearest obstacle, an opponent can station himself in a position of defence alongside the side line. No part of his body, however, must break the plane of the side line. The majority of our courts are not of this type and in these instances a broken line, three feet from the side line, should be marked on the court. Opponents must be behind this line. The thrower must not break the line with his feet or the plane of the line with his hands before releasing the ball, and the ball must be thrown and not just handed over to a team mate who may be chasing past.

FREE THROWS

Some mention has been made of the division of duties at a free-throw situation, but sufficient emphasis has not yet been placed on the importance of co-operation between the two officials and the calm but efficient approach they must show at these times. Whenever a whistle is blown, the officials must quickly exchange glances so that the signals can be noted and the reason for the stoppage of play understood. If a personal foul is to be followed by a free throw or if there is a technical foul, the officials change sides and consequently change duties. They do not rush to do this, but each official will have it uppermost in his mind. The official who 'called' the foul will be busy with his signals to the player concerned and to the table, and whilst he is doing this, the other official should get hold of the ball. Immediately these tasks have been performed, each official takes the position, and accepts the responsibility of his colleague. The recommendations which apply during normal officiating still apply at the free throw, namely the trailing official concentrates on the ball holder and the flight of the ball and the leading official watches the players off the ball. Before the free throw is taken, the stage has to be set. The free official ensures that the players are lined up around the free-throw lane in accordance with the rules. When he is satisfied that everything is in order he indicates this to the active official. He then moves back, proceeding to his left to a point near to the edge of the free-throw lane but about two feet out of the court itself. From here he should have a satisfactory view of all the players grouped around the free-throw area.

The active official in control of the ball indicates by finger signal the number of shots to be attempted, taking care to remain outside the restraining circle at the free-throw line. When he is satisfied that all is in order he glances at the scorer to ensure that no further signals are forthcoming, steps into the circle, hands the ball to the free thrower and retreats smartly two or three paces. The deliberate action of stepping into the circle clearly indicates to the scorer when the ball actually becomes alive as required by the game rules.

The active official raises one or two arms vertically to indicate the number of free throws. He is now responsible for the free thrower, the line and flight of the ball, signalling to the table, and for giving some indication to the free official that players may rebound if the ball is to remain in play.

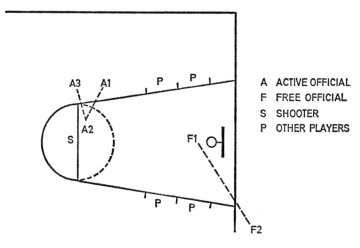

A   ACTIVE OFFICIAL
F   FREE OFFICIAL
S   SHOOTER
P   OTHER PLAYERS

8. Organization at a free throw

It is recommended that as soon as the ball hits the ring or backboard the raised hand be dropped smartly to give this indication. There are a whole series of laws governing movement during a free throw and these must be thoroughly learned, and inexperienced officials should practise free-throw situations to ensure that their reactions are quick and accurate. It is a very good point also to officiate during several games with the same co-official. In this way there can be discussion regarding the effectiveness of various signals and a system can be worked out which will make for efficiency and speed at free throws.

If the personal foul is to be followed by a throw in, the officials do not change sides, but they should co-operate nevertheless in getting the ball back into play quickly. Again they do this by the official who has called the foul controlling the signalling, and the other official obtaining the ball and having it ready for immediate use either by himself or his colleague.

On all occasions following personal fouls or technical fouls the signal is given by the official for the timekeeper to stop the clock. This should be remembered and, at the resumption of play, a signal for starting the clock must be given.

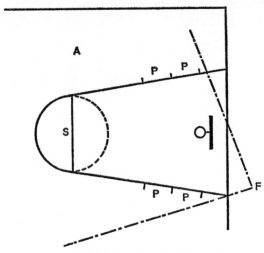

9. Position of officials for administration of free throw

During free-throw situations, there are often 'requests for sub-stitutes'. On these occasions and in fact during all occasions of substitutions the nearer official is responsible for beckoning the players on to the court. He ascertains the number of the man to be substituted and then it is a simple matter to see that the correct man leaves the court. Substitutions can prove to be chaotic if this simple procedure is not observed and, like all actions taken by the officials, substitutions should be done in an efficient and business-like manner.

It is especially important that the work done by the officials during periods when the clock is stopped is performed in the correct manner. On these occasions the officials become the focal point of attention by both the spectators and the players, and slip ups or bad handling of the situation tend to mark down the referee and the umpire as inefficient.

THE IMPORTANCE OF THE LAST FEW MINUTES

During the last few minutes of play in the second half, there is often a complete change of standard and style of play in the game itself. If the score has mounted evenly there will be an air of excitement amongst the spectators and a higher degree of nervous tension shown by the players. Tempers may become frayed and ugly situations develop unless the officials maintain cool control over the match. The officials may have had to work particularly hard throughout the game and even though they may be feeling tired, the chief testing time has still to come. They should, therefore, be especially careful during this period and should be completely conversant with the rules and on the lookout for the visible sign denoting that the last few minutes have begun.

It is an excellent idea periodically to glance at the clock during game stoppages in the last few minutes of play. This is especially important for the trailing official since he must make a particular note of the ball's actual location when time is up. Many officials tend to breathe a sigh of relief when the final signal goes and this may be because there are so many extra things to be taken into consideration during the closing stages. After the whistle has gone, however, there is still work to be done. The official timepiece must be checked and then the following sequence of events undertaken.

1. Scorer finalizes the score sheet. When this has been done and balanced the scorer signs the sheet.

2. The timekeeper signs the sheet.

3. The court officials check the sheet, the umpire signs.

4. The referee signs, confirms the score, and by this action he severs all connection with the game.

If there is provision for the captains to sign the sheet, then they should do so before the umpire and referee.

When the game is completed, the officials should not enter into argument with players or spectators regarding their decisions. If a question is asked by a player in a gentlemanly way, then a truthful answer should be given and no attempt should be made to bluster out of an awkward situation. The player who seeks information in an aggressive or a sneering way should be completely ignored.

It is wrong to be over friendly with a team before, during or after a game and if it is possible the officials should change in a separate room to the other players.

Every official must be prepared to give freely of time, money, energy and to a lesser degree his health and family life in pursuit of his hobby. What can he expect in return for this? There is little or no financial reward, certainly no gain, a little praise, few thanks but more criticism than most other men are likely to receive. If, however, the referee remembers his training, learns to eliminate his faults and progresses gradually without fuss and push he will become respected by others in the game and will be looked upon for leadership.

The better official will make lasting friends amongst players and coaches alike. The moment he assumes control, his games will settle down on to an even keel with the players, as one man, attempting to play the game within the rules, knowing that they have a fair judge on the sideline ready to penalize the wrong-doers and if necessary to protect the innocent. All his decisions must be made with confidence, and once made he must be firm in awarding the correct penalty.

Although at times it is tempting to offer criticism to a fellow official, it is wrong to behave in this way. Officials see the game from an entirely different angle to players and spectators, and even competent officials sitting with the spectators will not be on the lookout for those things which the man with the whistle is watching.

All good officials pay particular attention to the approved code of signals; they indicate their decisions clearly and keep the game in progress with the minimum of fuss and waste of time. They must be interested in their job and alert on all occasions. They should also be pleasant without being unduly familiar, and with this attitude they can hustle the players into the required positions without resorting to sergeant-major tactics.

To be a successful referee the following points are all-important; a thorough knowledge of the rules, good all-round ability, courage, sound judgement and a love of the game.

TABLE OFFICIATING

This is an art in itself. So much so that the A.B.B.A. has instituted a separate award for scoring and timekeeping for which I am the present administrator. The scorer's job is most complex and to produce a satisfactory score sheet he must carry out the following.

BASKETBALL OFFICIATING

Before the game he enters the game details, i.e. venue, time, opponents, referee, umpire etc. He also fills in the team details, e.g. players, captain, coach and preferably lists the players in number order. During the game, he records the points scored as a running total, the player scoring and the time of scoring. He also records the free throws made and missed, and all fouls committed identifying the fouls as ordinary, shooting, intentional, technical or disqualifying, at the same time indicating to everyone the number of fouls charged on a player as they occur.

The scorer must know the correct procedure for substitution and when to sound the signal. Under present rules, substitutions are permitted whenever the whistle sounds, but if a violation has been called, only the team putting the ball into play may initially substitute. If this occurs then the other team may also substitute, so the scorer must exercise care in this situation. The scorer must not signal when the ball becomes alive, however, as indicated in previous paragraphs.

At the end of the game the scorer finalizes the score sheet. He does this by entering the score, the name of the winning team, crossing out unused fouls and time-outs and obtaining signatures as indicated in paragraphs headed 'The importance of the last few minutes'.

The timekeeper has to stop the clock every time the whistle blows under present rules and start it again as follows:

(i) Out of bounds on the sideline following a foul or violation, when the ball touches the first player on court.

(ii) Following a successful free throw when the ball is put into play from the end line, the clock starts when the ball touches the first player on court. If the shot is not successful and the ball is to remain in play the clock starts when the ball is touched by the first rebounder provided that the ball has hit the ring.

At any jump ball the clock starts after the ball has reached its highest point when it is tapped by the first jumper.

6

THE SELECTION AND TRAINING OF SCHOOL REPRESENTATIVE TEAMS

by K. G. CHARLES

The selection of the best team is an extremely difficult task, especially when the chosen team is to remain together during the greater part of the season. Selectors must do their work properly or they may become dissatisfied with the personnel who have been picked out. Initially, therefore, the people concerned with selection must be capable of recognizing potential ability. They must remember that certain players who look good at trials fade away under the pressure of later matches, and other players who were initially not accepted may become real towers of strength.

How then can the best material be drafted into the training squad and what special points must selectors have in mind during trial games? These are some of the important questions to be answered, and an equally vital one concerns the general organization of the trial itself. The occasion on which the selection is made must be completely fair otherwise the players cannot be properly examined. The selectors must work to an organized system, and the coaches who will be responsible for team production must consider that the chosen players will blend into the programme of practice and style of play envisaged for the whole team.

There are two usually accepted methods of staging trials; one is the inter-area or inter-school game and the other is the conditioned game where players can perform in varying squads against different opponents. Both methods have their weaknesses. During inter-school games, the coaches tend to give undue prominence to their first five and, furthermore, the coaches dictate the pattern of play using the method best suited for the success of their own team. Consequently, they may not adopt man-to-man defence and instead rely on zone, even though man-to-man is the best indication of an individual player's defensive potential. In straightforward team *v.* team play, the ability of players may not be shown in true perspective, for the reasonable player when up against a weak opponent may appear to be remarkably good.

Conditioned games are much fairer, for all the players can be adequately put through their paces. Good attackers can be matched up with good defenders; the capable small lad can be put up against the average big lad and a truer comparison of ability can be explored.

Neither method, however, leaves much room for the nervous and inexperienced player who may have the power to be great but who for the time being has not the match temperament for trials. However, at national level, time and money tend to dictate the method, and where funds are low the trial lasting for one session sometimes has to suffice. It is essential, therefore, that the selectors are competent and efficient, well experienced in basketball and capable of judging aright.

Within a county or district, when more time is available, selectors would be well advised to work on the lines of the second method and choose a large training squad which will eventually be whittled down into a good team.

The numbers in the training squad, as opposed to a team, can vary. Some coaches prefer to work with ten players; others as many as sixteen or eighteen. What is really important is that selected players should be advised that they will only make the team proper by their showing at subsequent training sessions. In this way, players can be kept on their toes, for they must work hard, efficiently and consistently during the training programme to qualify for a place in the team. This method will also leave room for the inclusion of other players at a later stage, if necessary.

ADVICE TO SELECTORS

If a coach is to build up a well-balanced team he must be given

105

boys of wide potential. To this end the selectors should be looking for the following in each trialist.

1. *Ability in fundamentals*

Shooting—versatility of great advantage. He should not be a one-shot player. Every player should be able to perform with reasonable success the lay-up shot, right and left handed, the set shot up to and beyond a twenty-foot distance and the jump shot. If in addition to these shots he is good at the hook shot and the pivot shot he will have extra claims to a place.

Dribbling. An important fundamental that must not be ignored! A player should be able to make ground at speed whilst dribbling; he should have the skill to defend the ball without necessarily ending the dribble; he must know how to dribble the ball with purpose whilst setting up a play.

10. Dribbling and controlling

Ball Handling. A player must have the ability to make accurate and direct passes, and receive passes under many situations, e.g. fast breaks, set plays, or continuity plays. All too often teams lose a position of advantage because of the carelessness and poor ball handling of individual players.

Footwork. The ability to stop and start, change direction and pace and not infringe the travelling rules are vital assets. A player should be able to pivot with purpose in order to protect the ball or to get into a more favourable position to pass or to shoot. Here again, pivoting is generally weak in this country.

Individual defensive skill. The knowledge of the basic positions and stance of man-to-man defence are a 'must'. The proper application of this knowledge can only be acquired by a great deal of work on man-to-man principles. It is a fallacy that zone defence should be the first defence to be taught to learners. This is the root of many team defensive problems that develop at a later stage.

Rebounding. Good rebounders, particularly attacking rebounders, are rare, and selectors should be constantly on the search for players who have the ability and determination to master this fundamental. It is not an easy skill to acquire, for a player, as well as being a good ball handler and good at footwork, must have a fine sense of timing.

2. *Aggressiveness.* This quality is required at all times and can often make up for weaknesses in the accepted fundamentals. Aggressive teams can completely unbalance teams of far greater superiority in fundamentals and team plays. A player who will never give up, no matter what the score, who will 'push' himself to switch back and forth from defence to attack, is worth a great deal to any coach. Perhaps the greatest exponent of this is Alan Tillot, former Great Britain and England Captain. He has been known to pull his team from mediocrity into a first-rate fighting unit by his own aggressiveness.

3. *Height of player.* This may cause many raised eyebrows, but I firmly believe that, given the time, a coach can make a good basketball player out of a big man, despite early impressions of hopelessness. At national level, however, with perhaps only a few training sessions available, this consideration can only be made where players of equal ability, but varying height, are involved— then the obvious choice is the big man.

4. *Temperament of player.* Most important of all is the temperament of the player, not easily distinguished in trials, but nevertheless requiring careful observation. The player's attitude to coaching must also be considered. There is no room in this sport for the player who will not listen and carry out his coach's instructions implicitly. This does not mean that players cannot express their own opinions, in fact some coaches encourage team members to give their views at pre-game and mid-game tactical sessions. When the decision is made, however, it is the coach's decision and the player must carry it out.

5. *Fitness.* Basketball demands all-round fitness if championship level is to be attained. It is hard to create an accurate impression of the necessary standard but a general impression is that very few players in England are really fit to withstand forty playing minutes of a hard-pressing game. Many of our international players have spasms of brilliance which last a few minutes and then they fade away; the reason would appear to be a lack of fitness. Many basketball games are won or lost in the closing seconds of the match and the player who can still find the energy to command his backboards and to sink the vital foul shot or the unexpected lay-up is a most valuable team member. It is worth mentioning that international players from the Continent spend 50 per cent of their time getting and keeping fit—our fitness aim is far too low.

All these qualifications are difficult to judge. They need the eye of an experienced coach, and it may be that the best selection committees are those that contain the most qualified and experienced coaches. Generally, administrators, unless they are coaches, do not make good selectors, for they are so often falsely impressed by the player who makes crude baskets, at the expense of the better fundamentalist.

It is useful to call upon some aids to assist in selection, and here we can learn a lot from the American statisticians. With my squads I adopt several statistical methods, some of which are still in an experimental stage.

PLANNING THE PROPER TRAINING PROGRAMME

To plan the proper training programme, the coach must know how to organize efficiently the time he has at his disposal. The teacher, coaching a schools' representative team, has an added problem for he will probably be faced with a change of at least 60–100 per cent of the personnel every year, so it is not possible to have a long-term progressive programme.

Training times vary and in one year I was only able to have the national schools team together for one short weekend session—some seven or eight hours; the following year, two sessions of two days; and in the third year, three sessions—about twenty hours.

These sessions, whilst being extremely valuable to all concerned, still produced a major problem in themselves. This difficulty was centred on 'how to keep the boys giving maximum effort all the time?' The overall low rate of physical fitness meant that they could not have gone on any longer in individual sessions, even if time had been available. Fatigue set in far too early.

Coaches of county and district teams, however, would have more time at their disposal. In one season, I had twenty sessions of two hours with my county team. The sessions started early in October and continued until the following March. Despite the fact that I was dealing with some boys of lesser ability, I was able eventually to coach them in more advanced plays. In many ways I achieved greater team strength with this group than with the national team; five made the E.S.B.B.A. team and four figured in the first five of the same team—it was this team which convincingly won the national championships.

Once the available time has been calculated, it is then necessary to consider where the programme can be started. Here the coach is faced with probably the major difficulty and this is the lack of ability in certain essential fundamentals. This point I make with all humility and with the greatest respect for my fellow colleagues of the coaching fraternity. A considerable amount of very valuable work is put in by coaches around the country. They have not the backing and support of a national scheme and too often they are reduced, partly through the limited time at their disposal and partly through inexperience, to the coaching of a bare handful of fundamentals and a few team tactics. Hence, boys with great potential make the national team at present, only to hold back progress by their limited knowledge of tactics.

In arriving at the outline of the training programme, provision must be made for the following:

(*a*) Fitness training.

(*b*) Training in fundamentals.

(*c*) Training in team tactics and plays.

When time is limited, the coach tends to concentrate more on section (*c*) and adopt tactics and plays to suit the experience of the squad available.

(*a*) *Fitness training.* Much of the fitness training, if not all, can be carried out by the boy at home or at his school, and needs little observation from the coach. The coach should, however, give the players specific directions, and he should seek the co-operation of staff members of the boy's own school to see that the planned schedule is maintained. During the work itself, emphasis should be placed upon speed of movement and swift reaction. Stamina must be improved, together with jumping ability, both high and long; weight putting, using both left hand and right hand, should be included.

Activities

1. Short sprints—thirty yards—with *starting gun*.
2. Winders—three to four laps—for stamina. Jog, stride and sprint cycles, increasing length of sprint as stamina builds up.
3. High jumping—movements are allied to basketball movements in many ways.
4. Long jumping.
5. Weight training (under the direction of a qualified person).
6. Putting the weight—with both left and right hand.

A very interesting and important point regarding this athletic prowess is that from the ten members of the national schools' team in 1961, one was a full international athlete, two were national junior champions at their events, and seven were county or district champions.

(*b*) *Training in fundamentals.* Here again the player's school-master-coach can play an important part, which should improve both the coach's ability and the boy's playing ability.

For training and practice in shooting, an Individual Player's Record Card, as set out in Fig. 1, can be very valuable. This keeps a record of progressive training, and encourages the player to give regular attention to an important aspect of his work. The coach decides the type of shot and the maximum number of attempts, depending on the position of the player and the part he will play in the offence of the team. It is not suggested that every player must attempt every shot on the card, but if he is sufficiently dedicated and can find the time, he will attempt them all. Basketball is a game where a player needs as many strings to his bow as

FIG. 1

INDIVIDUAL PLAYER'S RECORD CARD

Name ....   *Date of birth* ....

School/Club ....

Shot	Position from	Max.	6/7/60	7/7/60	8/7/60	9/7/60	Max.
Right-hand lay-up	Right	20	14	13	15	19	20
Left-hand lay-up	Left	30	21	23	20	24	35
Lay-up	Centre	20	17	16	17	16	15
One-hand set	Centre	40	23	19	22	25	40
	Right	30	17	20	21	24	30
	Left	30	19	17	28	23	30
Two-hand set	Centre	30	20	20	21	20	25
	Right	30	19	21	21	17	30
	Left	30	19	12	15	16	35
Two-hand overhead	Centre	30	20	21	21	20	35
Right-hand hook	Right	50	35	34	33	38	50
Left-hand hook	Left	50	21	19	17	12	60
Jump	Right	40	21	17	19	21	40
	Left	40	11	15	15	13	45
Pivot (turn around)	Centre	30	9	9	9	9	30*

Return your card after each session. Remember the old saying:

PRACTICE MAKES PERFECT

INSTRUCTIONS FOR SHOOTING PRACTICE

Take your time. Think. Relax. Shoot.

LAY-UPS
No underhand lay-ups—bad habit.
Jump high.
Keep your thumb down.

ONE-HAND SET
Put the ball on the non-shooting hand.
Place your shooting hand at the back of the ball.
Shoot right up on your toes.
Follow through.

TWO-HAND SET
Keep your thumbs at the back of the ball.
Look at the ring over the ball.

JUMP
Remember, jump straight up.
Take the ball up to full stretch, then shoot.

HOOK
Turn your opposite shoulder towards the basket.
Look at the basket.
Hook the ball right over your head.

PIVOT
Keep the ball well protected and you will find your opponents are powerless to prevent the shot.

possible and to be very good at only one type of shot soon makes him relatively easy for an opponent to cope with.

A player should be proficient in two or three of the shots listed on the chart and be encouraged in all ways to develop his favourite shots.

During the individual practice sessions, a record is kept of all the shots made. The coach will then adjust the maximum number of attempts, as he sees weaknesses showing up, e.g. if a player is very weak with a shot, like the jump shot from the left, the coach will increase the number of attempts.

Although shooting is vitally important it is equally essential that regular practice should be done in dribbling, catching, passing, pivoting, stopping and starting, etc. Here it is not quite so simple to set down a training schedule, but with a little thought and ingenuity a series of tests can be evolved which demand proficiency in these various aspects. The player can then test himself against the clock whilst performing these skills, and so improve his technique. Such tests as the McCloy Revision of Edgren Basketball Test[1] can be usefully adapted, to come within the scope of the schedule. The element of competition, player against player or player against clock, must be present in order to maintain efficiency in practice. It is not sufficient, nor appetizing enough to a player, to tell him to dribble about the court for five minutes. When tests are applied, care must be taken to ensure that the measurements are standardized if they are to be used fairly when comparing individuals. It is very encouraging to watch the determination with which players face these tests, when they realize that they have a chance to prove themselves in front of their team mates. Incidentally, the good-hearted jesting by the observing players helps to build up the team spirit.

As far as defensive work is concerned, the best advice a coach can give a player is to play as many one-on-one games as possible. In this way the player should improve his defensive and offensive work, and his powers of summing up his opponent.

(*c*) *Training in team tactics and plays.* For the most part, this aspect can only be carried out during the team training sessions,

[1] *Tests and Measurements in Health and Physical Education,* McCloy and Young, p. 325.

in the presence of the county coach. The coach should consider the ability of the players he has at his disposal and then decide on the tactics that will best suit them.

It is essential, however, that every team is acquainted with the following aspects of play:

1. TEAM DEFENCE

(a) *Man-to-man defence*. The importance of man-to-man defence has been stressed as an essential part of basic training. From the usual positions taken up in this defence it is suggested that the team first learns a half-court press. In this way the fact that all the team crashes back under its own basket as soon as possession of the ball is lost will help the weaker members of the team, and decrease the chances of frequent fast breaks. As the team gains experience they can be coached not to go back so far into a position of defence and the full court press can be introduced. This is of considerable use when baskets are needed badly, particularly during the closing seconds of the game.

(b) *Zone defence*. The 2:1:2 zone defence is now recognized as the most successful in this country and is widely used. It provides the most efficient coverage of the defence area.

2. TEAM OFFENCE

Long periods of training are necessary if the coach is to develop the use of set offensive plays. Since this amount of time is not usually available, the usual method of offence is known as 'free basketball'. This does not mean that the attack is disorganized, but rather that a degree of latitude is allowed to players provided that they work on accepted moves within the framework of a 1:3:1 attack formation.

The team is given various options to practise using set shots, screen plays, post plays, pivot plays and fast breaks. It is then a question of the players recognizing the right opportunity and using an effective play with which they are acquainted.

Briefly, we naturally try to make a *fast break* from the moment we gain possession of the ball for this is a very successful manœuvre in the hands of school teams. The greatest stress must be placed, however, on the positioning of the receiver of the first pass. Many a fast break is destroyed because a pass is thrown too early or is wrongly directed towards the centre of the court. The best position in which to receive the pass is near the side lines, and the rebounder is instructed to look there first of all. This is the least likely place to find an opponent and the best place for the initial pass.

If the attack is slow and the opponents' defence has been set, we then take up the positions, as in Fig. 2, for the 1:3:1 attack formation.

FIG. 2

Movement of post player

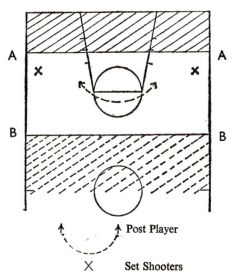

↑ Post Player

✕   Set Shooters

The pivot player uses the area between the end line and line A, which cuts through the second stub of the free-throw lane.

The post player and the two set shooters set up in the area between lines A and B. The post player will move along a path, as illustrated, cutting across the top of the free-throw lane. Most of his initial work will be done with his back to the basket. The set shooters select the positions from which they are able to shoot with confidence at the first opportunity. Many set shooters in American squads are directed by the coach to spend the greatest part of their shooting practice making set shots from that spot.

The safety man controls that area from line B to his rear court.

Opportunities that could be used with success are numerous, but here are a few generally accepted ones.

(a) The safety man makes a two-hand set shot, over the screen of the post player.

(b) The safety man, who is usually the best ball handler in the team, passes to a set shooter, who attempts a one-hand set shot.

(c) The safety man passes to a set shooter, who feeds the post player and cuts for a return hand-off pass, and an attempted lay-up.

(d) A feed from the safety man to the post player, who will pass to the cutting pivot player under the basket.

(e) The set shooter passes to the pivot player, and then moves in to set an inside screen for the pivot player to make a jump shot.

The basic set-up of that 1:3:1 attack formation is again valuable for its favourable rebounding positions, since any three players of the attack can move in without great difficulty to gain the offensive rebound.

To make the team efficient in these manœuvres and to give practice in these options, emphasis during training should be placed on the following movements.

(a) Screens, inside and outside.

(b) Criss-cross plays.

(c) Post plays.

(d) Pivot plays.

3. SET PLAYS FROM DEFINITE SITUATIONS

Many extra points are gained from well-organized set game situations, but when training time is short, practice in these movements must be restricted. Nevertheless, it is advisable to cover at least one play from each of the main situations:

(a) Tip off at centre.

(b) Jump balls from both the offensive and defensive circles.

(c) Free-throw situations—offensive and defensive.

(*d*) Side line out of bounds.

Here again, the coach will decide the play to use, depending on the potential of his team. It will only take a short time to devise these set plays but it is advisable to maintain simplicity of movement and to ensure that all the players have perfect knowledge with every move.

Blending the team and team development. To bring together a number of individuals, each with his own weaknesses and, probably, a different coaching background, and mould those same individuals into a team unit, is no easy task. The coach must use tact and common sense in his approach and, at the same time, he must make certain demands of his team. The manner in which this is done will differ from individual to individual, and will depend upon the temperament of both the coach and the player. There are no hard and fast rules although with school teams the position is somewhat easier because of the traditional attitude and approach of teacher to pupil.

Whatever method is adopted, the aim should be to create a unit that has a healthy respect for the coach and also a true sense of loyalty. In my opinion, the coach must be the master of the team and I am convinced that our position in sport could be improved by more emphasis on the importance and value of the good coach. There is still plenty of room for freedom of action and initiative within the bounds of a well-coached team. The team does not necessarily become a number of robots carrying out mechanical movements under the strict instruction of the coach. The coach bases his instruction on an assessment of both sides and the use of his team's best potential.

A player then will show his loyalty by his willingness and readiness to carry out the decisions of the coach to the last letter. The appointment of a good team captain will contribute much to the success of the team and the co-operation of the players, for he will encourage, persuade and coerce his team mates, especially when the run of play is against them. The best example I had of this occurred when one of my senior players came across at a time-out, when the team was trailing in points, and said that a certain method of defence would not work effectively. Before I could utter a word, the team captain and the other three players on court immediately disagreed and insisted on being given another chance to prove it was possible. The former player accepted this, and all five returned to the game, as if fired with a new determination. Need I say, they went on to win the game convincingly.

This loyalty to the coach must be carried over to the rest of the team and must surpass any feeling of self-glorification. Naturally, every player must be enthusiastic and itching to be one of the players on court, but not at the expense of failures by another team mate. If a player makes a mistake, the rest of the team, particularly those on the bench, should help him to overcome any resulting feeling of nervousness by encouragement, rather than by uttering words of scorn. A coach from his own side must not expect to command respect and loyalty just because he is the coach, senior member, or teacher; he must win it by common-sense actions, by demanding effort of his team, and showing respect for them.

The best team will be the one that is well balanced in all its fundamentals, and one in which every player can shoot with a certain accuracy, when necessary. To this end, all the players should be encouraged to shoot whenever the opportunity arises, and not just to seek out the team's best scorer and pass to him. There is great merit in being an unselfish player who gives many valuable assists, but all players must also be blessed with a certain shooting potential if every opportunity is to be taken.

The problems of discipline and coach-player relationship are lightened by regular practice sessions. The coach gets to know his players and the limits he can go in making his 'demands'; and the players meet each other on more social terms and many a strong friendship is formed.

This situation is more acute with national teams, although in certain instances the force of circumstances has been of great help. From our own experience, we had to rely on some occasions upon the generosity of parents to accommodate boys who lived farther afield. As a result we discovered friendships growing up between the players, and these friendships spread throughout the team. The weekend sessions helped considerably to foster a most friendly atmosphere and this applied even more where some social get-together was included, e.g. a visit to an ice-hockey match on the Saturday evening.

SCHOOL REPRESENTATIVE TEAMS

In preparation for the big games, training games were arranged with local league sides for the Under-18 years group, and with strong school teams or junior clubs for the Under-15 years groups. These games, whilst having certain drawbacks, helped the players to put into practice the plays which they had learnt in training sessions. It is in such games as these that use could be made of score charts and other analytical aids.

FIG. 3

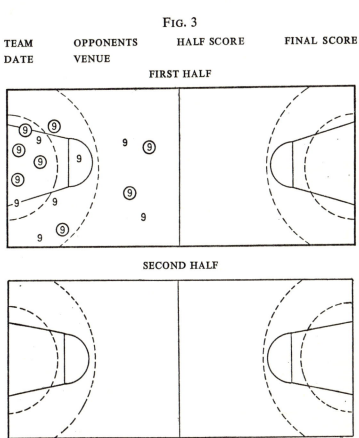

TEAM   OPPONENTS   HALF SCORE   FINAL SCORE
DATE   VENUE

FIRST HALF

SECOND HALF

Fig. 3. *Scoring chart* (*both teams*). Record the number of the player at approximate spot of shot, e.g. 9. Circle it only if he scores, e.g. 9.

Fig. 4. *Summary of shots.*

Long shots—over 20 feet.

Medium shots—between 10 and 20 feet.

Short shots—under 10 feet.

Free throws can also be recorded.

In this way a record of percentages can be kept and these results will increase the enthusiasm of the team.

FIG. 4

Summary of Shots

TEAM   OPPONENTS   VENUE   DATE

SUMMARY OF SHOTS

Player	No.	Time played	Long		Medium		Short		Totals		Per cent	Free Throws	
			S	B	S	B	S	B	S	B		S	B
TEAM TOTALS													

S—Shots attempted   B—Baskets made

Fig. 5. *Court record.*

Rebounds:

Offensive—off opponents' backboard.

Defensive—off own backboard.

Rebounding is an aspect of the game that is very weak in this country. Records encourage the players to work harder at this fundamental.

Losses:

Passes—faulty pass to colleague which goes astray or is intercepted.

Violation—violating a rule, e.g. double dribble, travelling, etc.

Ball handling—fumbling and loss of ball by receiver. The number of failures in these aspects is considerable and the records are useful in bringing back to earth the high scorers with fundamental weaknesses.

FIG. 5

Court Record

Player	No.	REBOUNDS		LOSSES			RECOVERIES		
		Offensive	*Defensive*	*Passes*	*Violation*	*Ball hand*	*Interception*	*Tie ups*	*Jump ball*

OPPONENTS　　　VENUE　　　DATE　　　SCORE

Recoveries:

Interception—intercepting a pass between opponents.

Tie-ups—forcing an opponent into a position where he can make little progress; sometimes compelling him to make a violation.

Jump ball—held ball situation.

After the training games are over, I discuss the game with the team and draw attention to major weaknesses, both team and individual. At all times I encourage positive criticism and suggestions from the team, and some very useful and common-sense ideas come to light as a result.

The Training Sessions

Most training sessions should last for two hours and the plan which is given is based upon this time factor. The long weekend sessions of training with the national team are more speedily progressive and will not really serve as a good example.

The training session is divided up into three major parts:

1. Fundamentals and associated drill (50 minutes).
2. Team tactics and plays (50 minutes).
3. A condition game (20 minutes).

1. FUNDAMENTALS AND ASSOCIATED DRILLS

This serves very well as an opener to the session, for team members, like club members, often arrive at different times. As the gymnasium is not occupied by any other group, no time is lost and useful drills are started straight away. The drills are well known and simple, but there is plenty of variety from session to session. In most cases the drills will be selected as part of the build-up for the team tactics and plays section.

(*a*) *Rogues.* A dribbling drill. More than half of the players should be given a ball, which they can dribble freely in a prescribed area. They must, however, work according to normal basketball rules. Those without a ball attempt to steal one by touching a ball.

(*b*) *Ten consecutive passes.* A team has to make consecutive passes without the other side *touching* the ball.

(*c*) *Pepper-potting.* Two balls are given to five or six players lined up to face one player. The balls are passed to the single player, who feeds them back so that they rotate along the line.

(*d*) *Truck and Trailer.* Working in pairs with one ball. The dribbler moves forward, followed by his partner, then stops, pivots around and hands off to his partner, who cuts close by. He then becomes the trailer.

(*e*) *Lay-up drill.* Working from both the right-hand side and the left-hand side.

(*f*) *Rebounding war*. Three or four players compete against each other at one basket to be the first to make a given number of points. Whilst deliberate fouling is out, there will be a certain amount of contact which should be ignored.

2. TEAM TACTICS AND PLAYS

We usually work at a revision of a system of attack or defence practised in an earlier session, and then introduce one new system. We will suppose that the aim of the session is to improve the rebounding strength of the team. The first part would be a revision of the rebounding paths from the basic offensive set-up, that is 1:3:1. The squad would divide up and play half-court basketball. Each team would have five attempts at the basket and then the defending opponents would change to attack. In this case the attacking team would be instructed to miss with the first shot so that the offensive rebounders can get in and obtain possession of the ball.

The second stage would be the positioning of man-to-man defenders, in order to get into a favourable place for rebounding. They would be specifically instructed to guard their opponents closely all the time, and only to move in for the rebound when the player they are marking moves in. If the attacking player cuts to the left of the defender, the defender should pivot on his left foot and move into the basket, hence keeping the opponent 'on his back'. This is the movement usually known as 'blocking out'.

3. A CONDITIONED GAME

For the conditioned game, the full court would be used. In addition to an observation of all rules, the players would be instructed that they *must* concentrate on the points stressed in section 2. Furthermore, in order to encourage rebounding, particularly at the opponents' backboard, the baskets would only be counted where an offensive rebounder touched it *immediately* it dropped out of the net, or was the first person to take possession of it.